Take the Next Step

LEADING LASTING CHANGE IN THE CHURCH

Lovett H. Weems, Jr.

Abingdon Press / Nashville

TAKE THE NEXT STEP
LEADING LASTING CHANGE IN THE CHURCH

Library of Congress Cataloging-in-Publication Data

Weems, Lovett H. (Lovett Hayes)
    Take the Next Step: leading lasting change in the church / Lovett H. Weems, Jr.
    p. cm. (Discoveries : insights for church leadership)
    Includes bibliographical references (p.   )
    ISBN 0-687-02084-0
    1. Christian leadership. I. Title.

BV652 .1.W443 2003
253—dc22

2003016817

03 04 05 06 07 08 09 10 11 12—10 9 8 7 6 5 4 3 2 1

MANUFACTURED IN THE UNITED STATES OF AMERICA

Take the Next Step

Leadership is helping God's people take the next faithful step.

Scott Cormode

Contents

Introduction

What Happens When the World Changes?

Stan Copeland is pastor of Lover's Lane United Methodist Church in Dallas, Texas, one of the largest churches in his denomination. Speaking at the seminary he attended about a year after going to Lover's Lane, he reflected on how ministry had changed in the fifteen or so years since he left seminary.

"During my seminary days," Stan recalled, "the watchword was 'change the world.' We were determined to reshape the world more in alignment with God's reign. Our faculty was committed to this goal. It all seemed quite simple and doable at the time. 'Change the world' was indeed our mantra."

"However," he continued, "no one of us—faculty or students—gave any attention to the question that would shape pastoral ministry in our generation: 'What do we do when the *world* changes?'"

Stan reflects the experience of many clergy today. Shaped and educated in a world of apparent givens about church and world, we followed our presumptions into one direction of ministry even as the world was changing and rendering our approaches to ministry less and less effective. We had set out to "change the world" from the sure foundation of the church's message and place in society. Then, the world changed in unexpected ways. No longer was the world a known object needing reform but rather an unknown entity needing, first, understanding. Likewise, the church that had been a source of answers scrambled to find ways to connect with new generational, social, cultural, and spiritual landscapes.

Stan went on to say that he is doing ministry in ways no one would have imagined when he began his ministry. Whether it is worship, youth ministry, education, or outreach, the dynamics have changed, at least for those congregations maintaining a vital ministry in today's world.

He illustrated the changed assumptions with an incident that had occurred the previous Sunday in a youth Sunday school class taught by his wife, Tammy. A student came faithfully to the class with all the identifying marks of his particular group, including blue hair going in all directions. He also wore each week a spike collar. On this particular Sunday, everything was as always with one major exception. The student did not wear the spike collar. When Tammy asked why he was not wearing the collar, the student gave a look of disbelief at the question. "Why," he said, "this is Easter." His tone of voice made it clear that he was surprised that his teacher did not have a sufficient sense of the sanctity of Easter to understand why he would dress differently for such a holy day. Yes, the world has changed!

The church and the world out of which Stan Copeland entered seminary no longer exist in many places and in many ways. Thousands of pastors such as Stan, and just as many congregations, are struggling today with the question that has perplexed the church through the ages at times of major social change, "What do we do when the world changes?"

Today is one of those classic best and worst of times for congregations. It is the worst of times because recent decades have not been good for many churches. Churches of some denominations have experienced a "disestablishment" of their traditional predominance in American religion. At the same time, the demographics of the traditional constituencies of these churches have worked against numerical growth through lower birth rates and higher death rates. Population mobility has left many long-existing congregations located in places where the population used to be. Despite population growth, some denominations pulled back in their commitment to new church starts. Some congregations operate in a seeming class captivity that makes it hard for them to reach out beyond their typical membership to the growing numbers of persons who are younger, more racially diverse, and less well off than their membership.

It is the best of times because we see examples of vibrant congregational ministry today that would not have been predicted even a few years ago and that give hope for the future. There are local churches that have grown to a size thought in the past to be impossible to achieve in the United States. The local church I attend began eleven years ago and has 11,000 members and constituents today, while proudly claiming its denominational identity and featuring both contemporary and traditional worship. There are other churches that have literally remade themselves to address the needs of their changed communities. Other churches are maintaining a stable ministry presence where every demographic indicator would have predicted that these churches would have died years ago. Still other churches, despite being much smaller in size than at their "heyday," now have a greater engagement in their communities than ever in their history. We are seeing new worship models that are reaching persons who had previously shown limited interest in the church.

Despite all the struggles facing long-existing congregations today, there are countless churches accomplishing their missions in ways never dreamed possible not many years ago. The common denominator is that all these vital churches have found ways to change to meet new situations.

Leadership is about change.

DIFFICULTY OF CHANGE

People don't want change. They just want things to get better.

Rosabeth Moss Kanter

But nothing is more fraught with danger than change. Everything about human and organizational life leads toward stability and not change. In human organizations the most powerful pull is always to keep change within a fairly narrow range. All human groups become uncomfortable when change goes beyond their zone of what is acceptable. "It's generally much easier to kill an organization than to change it substantially," claims one observer. "Organisms by design are not made to adapt . . . beyond a certain point."[1] Although this may overstate the point, it is surely true that there are limits to how much change all living organisms, including organizations of people, can endure without great stress on the system.

James O'Toole, in his fine book on leading change, contends that groups of people "resist change with all the vigor of antibodies attacking an intruding virus."[2] From the earliest anthropological studies to modern experience, he says, change in organizations is the exception, not the rule. In no case does it come about quickly or easily.

So, change leaders must begin by understanding that the natural inclination of all groups is to resist change, regardless of the merits or who we are. Such resistance is not so much a moral failure of the people in our churches as it is a gravitational pull of groups toward stability rather than change.

Churches share all the normal resistance of human organizations to change and perhaps bring more sources of resistance. Although not alone among institutions in stressing tradition, churches are clearly deeply rooted in tradition, not only a local congregation's history but also an ecclesial tradition and the centuries-long tradition of the Christian faith itself. Tradition is taken extremely seriously in the church. Churches are often not accustomed to change, or at least to thinking consciously about change.

"Is not the gospel unchanging?" some might ask. Even laity who work daily in arenas where anticipating and planning change is a way of life fail to sense the same priority for such attention to change in their churches. Church members also share with many in the larger society a weariness with change. Many have not been served well by larger societal changes. They seek in their churches a sanctuary from the struggles they face in life, dealing with changes beyond their control. The last thing they are eager for is change in the one place they can depend upon to be predictable and stable.

NECESSITY OF CHANGE

Any object at rest tends to remain at rest. An object in motion tends to remain in motion. Every action gives rise to an opposite reaction. Force equals mass times acceleration.

Sir Isaac Newton

As people of faith, we have no option but to change. Change is not for the sake of change but for the sake of God's will. We affirm that God has been active in our lives and in our congregations throughout the past. For that, we give thanks. We also believe that God is present in our lives and in our congregations today. For that, we celebrate every expression of God's presence with us. Yet, none of us or our congregations so fully represent the fullness of God's will in our past and in our present that we can say, "We are now everything God ever intended for us to be."

Not only do we believe that God has been in our past and is

in our present, we also affirm that God still has something in our future. God always has a "not yet" for us and for our churches. The key is to discover what God's preferred future is and to move toward that vision. We cannot become what we need to be by remaining what we are. To say we must change is not to judge the past except to the extent that no state of things can be deemed as synonymous with God's ultimate will. It is out of God's work among us in the past that we are able to move forward and change for the future. It is with a deep sense of thankfulness that we turn in prayer to God, asking God to reveal to us that to which we are being called in the days ahead. Change is at its heart a theological issue. God has a future for us beyond all that we have known and experienced up to now. We are called to discern and pursue that future.

Although the challenge is change, the mandate is as old as the gospel. We are a people of repentance and conversion. We know that we serve a God of new life, new creation, and new humanity. We are pilgrims always seeking God's New Jerusalem on the horizon.

True conservatism and true progressivism are not two opposites: conservatives dislike "change," yet they as well as progressives want to grow; progressives dislike to "stand pat," yet they as well as conservatives want to preserve what is good in the present. But conservatives often make the mistake of thinking they can go on living on their spiritual capital; progressives are often too prone not to fund their capital at all.

Mary Parker Follett (1868–1933)[3]

We also know that change, though difficult, is possible. How many of us have experienced change in our own lives well beyond what we could ever have dreamed? The pages of history are filled with stories of individuals and congregations who became more than anyone could have expected. Indeed, we know from experience that God "by the power at work within us is able to accomplish abundantly far more than all we can ask or imagine" (Eph. 3:20).

So we begin with full awareness of the human resistance to change but also with an equal knowledge of human potential for renewal and change.

We also know that all living systems have the capacity to grow and deal with changing environments. Though not automatic, the potential is obviously present. Peter Senge uses a biological analogy for change. He draws from a famous biologist who said "history is a process of transformation through conservation. Nature preserves a small set of essential features and thereby allows everything else to change."[4] It is in this spirit that every generation of Christians seeks to preserve the essentials of the treasure of the gospel without idolizing the "earthen vessels" in which the gospel is carried and which from generation to generation must change.

CONGREGATIONS AND CHANGE

As environments change . . . it would seem a simple matter for a congregation to assess the changes, decide on a course of action, and implement new programs and strategies in response. That rarely happens....[F]amiliar patterns often blind congregations to the change in the first place. Once they recognize change, their ability to imagine the future is blunted by the weight of the past. And even valiant, imaginative efforts to change are made more difficult by expectations and assumptions long in place. The most common response to change, in fact, is to proceed with business as usual.

Nancy T. Ammerman[5]

The respected sociologist of religion Nancy Ammerman has studied hundreds of congregations from many traditions, locales, and sizes. She indicates that when the communities around churches change or when the needs of the people within the churches change, congregations have before them an array of options from which to choose as to how they will respond to these changed circumstances. However, the most common response by churches to a changed environment is to continue to do things the same way.[6]

It is as if the world has changed and no one notices. When what worked for these churches in responding to the needs of people in an earlier time fails to achieve the desired results now, most churches do more of what is not working and thus compound their difficulties. This tendency to respond to shifts in the environment by accelerating past activities might be thought of as *vigorous inertia*. The practice is universal across organizations, cultures, and history.

CHANGE THROUGH EVOLUTION OR REVOLUTION?

Talk of the world changing and of a church determined to continue doing business as usual seems to lead to the conclusion that radical change is needed. The language of "revolution" is sometimes used to describe what is necessary for the church to thrive in the changed world of today. Familiar charts contrast our time with previous eras. The case for revolutionary change appears logical given the new world in which we live. But I fear the rhetoric of radical change may have run ahead of the reality of how congregations function and change from one era to the next.

This is not so much to criticize those who pursue a more revolutionary approach to church change as it is to supplement their important insights. My encouragement to readers is not to make an ideological commitment to any one approach to change but to learn from every source what truth is there and draw upon those resources that fit one's particular situation. "Does it ring true?" is a more important question for any reader than "This is what someone said." There are clearly times and situations that call for a new and radically different beginning for a congregation. My sense is that such occasions are rare for existing congregations.

The issue is not big change versus little change. Scott Cormode defines the goal of leadership as "helping God's people take the next faithful step." What that means and how one gets there will be different for different congregations. One church's "next faithful step" may seem to others to be quite modest. Yet if they knew what that congregation had been through, they would realize immediately that the church's vision is indeed grand. The ultimate goal, whatever the approach, is the revitalization of congregations to be more fully bearers of the witness of Christ in their communities and beyond.

Successful and lasting change comes more through evolution than revolution. Some assume that, if real change is to take place in their congregations, they must adopt an entirely new theological and liturgical identity. Rarely is this the situation. There must be continuity for genuine change to take place—change that has integrity and staying power.

Someone who spends time in a number of different churches said recently, "You could go to a different church every Sunday for a long time and each week be at a church that is alive and vital." Although many churches are not responding well to their changed environments, it is also true that there is tremendous revitalization going on today within congregations of all sizes, denominations, and locations.

There are exciting "new paradigm" congregations creating their own distinctive culture and making paths where many churches have not gone before. There are also many congregations renewing themselves in continuity with their distinctive character and history. Such revitalized churches are of many different sizes and are found in every imaginable location. Some have demographic growth on their side while some are flourishing where virtually every other institution has closed.

Most existing congregations operate out of histories that will, of necessity, shape their futures, just as our own personalities and backgrounds shape our futures—even when those futures move in new directions. It is important for a church to renew out of its own distinctive culture and history. This involves, first, understanding the history and culture out of which a congregation operates, defining the current reality of the church and environment, and discerning God's vision for the next chapter of the congregation's story. Then the congregation moves to "take the next step" by living into the next chapter that is both new and fresh, but at the same time tied intimately with the "DNA" of the congregation.

CHANGE IS CHANGING

The *Harvard Business Review* has added a new feature in which, once a year, they present the key cutting edge ideas that have emerged in the field of management over the past twelve months. A recent article in this series on emerging concepts carried the intriguing title—"Change Is Changing." Acknowledging that thinking about change is changing, they report that many management experts say leaders "need the guts to say no to revolution." "Radical change," they explain, "can impose more stress on an organization than it can bear and end up destroying what makes [it] viable."[7] Eric Abrahamson calls for an appreciation of human resistance to change and advances the merits of "dynamic stability," an evolutionary rather than revolutionary process.[8]

Peter Drucker claims that leaders today are "upsetting people unnecessarily—not because there is too much change, but because leaders do not even try to emphasize the continuity."[9] Even those who champion more revolutionary models of change caution leaders to monitor just how much change their organizations can handle at any one time.

"Change looks revolutionary only in retrospect," according to Rosabeth Moss Kanter. "The connotation of change—an abrupt disjunction, a clean break—does not always match the reality of change."[10] The attention to dramatic revolutionary turnarounds bears little resemblance to the nature of change in most congregations. An evolutionary view of change may be less dramatic than grand transformation, but it is "also more inclusive, more realistic, and more hopeful for most people who care to make a difference in their worlds," says Debra E. Meyerson. She believes this more incremental approach "is also more reflective of how most real and lasting change occurs."[11]

To the outside observer, or even to participants looking back on an era of change, the accomplishment may appear more revolutionary than it did to the actual participants at the time it was taking place. There almost always are clear, if sometimes subtle, connections between what looks like revolutionary change and the culture and current circumstances, so that the effort has an "of course" quality for those involved directly.

People hear of a major change in a nearby congregation. They can hardly believe the news. They know how difficult, if not impossible, such a change would be in their similar congregations. Everyone is eager to know what is the elaborate strategy or key intervention that took place that forced such a change. However, when talking with some members of the church, people find nothing dramatic in the descriptions of what had happened. In fact, the congregants seem surprised by the special interest being shown. For them the change had come much more naturally than anyone on the outside can imagine because of dynamics unique to that congregation in that moment. What seemed revolutionary to other churches around them felt more evolutionary to those involved.

An evolutionary approach is not an argument for incremental change only. While all churches need to improve constantly all aspects of their ministry, evolutionary change goes well beyond such incremental improvements. The difference in an evolutionary model versus a revolutionary model is not in the size or scope of change. The distinguishing characteristic of evolutionary change is that it is clearly tied to the congregational story and culture. Greater change may result from this approach since the success rate for change efforts should be higher, given less congregational resistance.

IMPORTANCE OF LEADERSHIP

Leadership is "getting people to a place they would not get to on their own."

Bill Shore[12]

This book also presupposes the importance of leadership to church revitalization. There is one common denominator in virtually all examples of renewal—the presence of visionary spiritual leadership. This leadership goes well beyond clergy, but it is rare that real renewal comes without the prayerful and committed engagement of pastoral leadership.

The exact shape of that leadership will be as different as the personalities of people and congregations are. There is no "one size fits all" when it comes to leadership or to God's will for local churches. Effective spiritual leaders seek lessons and clues for their leadership and their churches from the examples of others, but they always remember that the important question is, "What is God most calling *us* to do in *our* situation?"

This book is written for those who want to be agents through whom God can work for new life in congregations of all kinds and circumstances. It is my prayer that something in this book will be just the word most needed to encourage the heart and guide the way for God's leaders.

Chapter 1
First Create Trust

We must be the change we seek to produce.
Gandhi

The ability to create trust is the foundational competency for effective change. When church leaders begin
reading supposedly secular books about leadership, it
is often a great surprise that the language used in the best of
the books seems to come from the vocabulary of the church.
Church leaders may expect to find elaborate grids, schemes,
and designs. Instead, the words that dominate have to do
with values and character. It soon becomes quite evident that
there is no way to talk about leadership without talking
about values, character, and relationships.

When I was a seminary president, I spent much time raising money. That is one thing seminary presidents are called
to do. Years ago I heard the statistic that major gifts tend to
come after a dozen or so visits, often by the president. I was
close to that statistical average with a woman in her nineties.
She had ample resources, no family, close ties to the church,
interest in our school, yet had never given a single gift. I
arranged yet another visit with her by scheduling a flight
with a lengthy layover in her city so I could take her to din-
ner, as was our usual pattern.

When I arrived at her home, she was not dressed to go
out. She indicated that she was not feeling well and perhaps
we could visit for a few minutes and then I could head back

to the airport. We talked briefly in her living room. Then, as I was standing at the door to leave, she said simply, "I trust you." Her words meant a great deal to me personally, as my regard for her had grown through the years. I also knew then that she wanted to provide significant support for the seminary; she left half of her estate for student scholarships.

That was the day I learned that the term *development* was no mere euphemism for "fund-raising." It became abundantly clear to me that people give out of trust, and that trust grows out of relationships and experiences that engender such trust.

A term sometimes used in communication theory is the "ethical proof" of the speaker. *Ethical proof* refers to the credibility that the hearers accord the speaker. When the ethical proof is high, the task of persuading the audience is not hard. When the ethical proof is neutral, the speaker has a more difficult time. When the ethical proof is negative, the speaker has an extremely difficult time persuading the audience. This concept means that the way the constituents perceive the leader is often much more important than the "facts" of the presentation.

So it is with the presence of trust and credibility between leaders and constituents. James Kouzes speaks of credibility as "credit-ability."[1] People are doing an analysis of our credibility all the time just as a bank might assess our credit worthiness. Indeed, credibility is the working capital of the leader. It is from the account of credibility that the leader draws to make possible creative change. Credibility is the foundation upon which all effective leadership builds.

A leader wins trust slowly, but can lose it quickly. Once lost, this trust is difficult to regain in that leadership setting. People may give us a leadership position through election or employment. However, the credibility needed to lead must be worked out among the people with whom we serve. It is trust from those with whom the leader works most closely that gives a leader the essential element of credibility.

TRUST REQUIRED FOR LEADERSHIP

A United Methodist bishop met with a group of seminary leaders recently to discuss his observations about the type of clergy leadership most needed by churches today. The bishop noted with disappointment that many clergy leaders appear not to give the time and attention required to develop trust relationships sufficient for effective leadership. What the bishop observes about clergy leadership is true of all leadership.

The level of trust that exists within an organization and toward leaders is crucial to the effectiveness of leadership. When trust is limited, it is difficult for progress to take place. Change requires a minimal level of trust. Some speak of a "trust threshold" or a "radius of trust." That describes the variations in trust we all experience in relation to individuals and groups. Over time we come to extend more trust to some people and organizations than to others.

Economists remind us that in societies where the "radius of trust" is limited to family and a few close friends, a strong and expanding economic life is difficult to achieve. Economic transactions require a certain level of trust. Lack of sufficient trust imposes something like a tax on all interactions that makes progress more difficult.[2]

This helps explain why in low-trust organizations, even modest change is hard to achieve. Conversely, in places where a high level of trust has been developed, remarkable change can be accomplished with a minimum of acrimony and delay.

The leadership challenge is to provide the "glue" to cohere independent units in a world characterized by forces of entropy and fragmentation. Only one element has been identified as powerful enough to overcome those centripetal forces, and that is trust.

James O'Toole[3]

COMPONENTS OF TRUST

Relationships

Relationships are the first imperative for trust. Warren Carter, Pherigo Professor of New Testament at Saint Paul School of Theology, describes characteristics that are central to leadership in the church in the New Testament, and names "relationships" as the first. Helen Doohan notes personal involvement with the people as a significant characteristic of Paul's leadership. The importance of relationships is seen in Paul's early leadership, described in First Thessalonians and developed more fully in later letters, in which he is intimately involved with the community, and his life is intimately bound together with theirs.[4]

It was relationships that provided the foundation for Paul to address pivotal issues. Relationships are more than ends in themselves for leaders. For Paul, involvement and relationship provided a context in which issues and questions could be placed and handled.[5] We are called to build relationships so that we can all better serve a common mission and vision. On the other hand, working on fulfilling a common purpose, with all its struggles, can be important in building strong and lasting relationships. One does not build positive relationships as a substitute for mission but to make mission possible. And on the way to fulfilling mission, new and even deeper relationships are discovered.

The sensitive and delicate relationship between an orchestra director and the members of the orchestra is a helpful reminder of the importance of relationship between leaders and those with whom they work. A strong bond must be established if leadership is to take place. A study of leaders in one professional field found that the number one reason leaders failed was an "inability to get along." "Poor interpersonal skills represent the single biggest reason for failure," the report said, "and the most crucial flaw to recognize and remedy."[6] A denominational executive spent a year visiting every local church in the state where he gave oversight. At the end of the year, when asked for any insights about clergy leadership that came to him from this experience, he said that the single most common source of difficulty for pastors was in their struggles around interpersonal relations within the congregation.

One of the distinguishing qualities of successful people who lead in any field is the emphasis they place on personal relationships.

Ronald A. Heifetz and Marty Linsky[7]

Clearly presence is a requirement for establishing strong and solid relationships. Absence does not "make the heart grow fonder" in congregational life. Just the opposite is true. Relationship building takes time, attention, and care. It was the late Tip O'Neill, former Speaker of the United States House of Representatives, who popularized the phrase "All politics is local."

Increasingly I am coming to believe that all leadership is local. There is a sheer presence required for effective leadership. Leaders must stay close to the people with whom they work and close to the details of what is happening in their setting of leadership. When too much time and emotional energy are being given to endeavors outside that setting of leadership, there is almost always a deterioration of the quality of relationships and leadership.

I remember being struck by a comment made by a nationally famous preacher who was speaking at our seminary. I remarked that he probably spent a great deal of time away from home doing such speaking. He indicated that he did not. He went on to tell about numerous weekly ties he has to congregational members and events and how he will rarely be away so as to have to miss one of them. Since that time I have noticed how closely great leaders stay connected to their local settings of leadership.

In the 1960s I heard the activist Saul Alinsky speak. A college student asked him about what the student might do to become a national social movement leader. Alinsky's answer was immediate and simple: "If you want to be a great leader, you must become a great leader in a local community." Yes, all leadership is local, and it begins with the bonding of leaders and constituents which is so critical to trust.

Before there are plans and programs, human relationships must be formed. Credibility is built on relationships. Although leaders normally can expect some basic acceptance from the group because of the leadership role, that is not an adequate relational basis for leadership at all. It is that strong bond that is required for leadership.

In fact, Kouzes and Barry Posner define leadership as "a reciprocal relationship between those who choose to lead and those who decide to follow." Margaret Wheatley makes clear the importance of relationships in her understanding when she says, "Relationships are everything."[8]

The first imperative for establishing and maintaining trust is the *quality* of relationships that are established by the leader. Therefore, the priority for a leader is to establish a relationship of trust and respect with the people with whom the leader is working. Everything depends on this bonding. We come to trust people we know. Building such relationships requires active presence. Since we come to trust people we know, whom do we know? We know people who are *there*. Proximity is the most important reason people talk to each other. Leaders are present and visible.

At the most basic level, we trust those who care about us.

We trust those who we believe understand our concerns and will act in a way that takes our needs into account. Trust develops from relationships that engender confidence and mutual respect. It is developed within the context of leadership in the day-by-day interactions with real people in actual circumstances. Paul speaks of authority being used for "building up" and not for "tearing down" (2 Cor. 13:10). Do people perceive us as caring about them and seeking what is best for them?

True leaders know it is not a matter of *appearing* to care. "Whom you would change," Martin Luther King, Jr., said, "you must first love." Secular writers make the same point in saying that just possibly "the best-kept secret of successful leaders is love."[9]

Character

A second imperative for trust is character. Character here means honesty and integrity that comes from consistency between one's words and actions. Behavior is the key. Even perceptions of inconsistency hurt trust. Perfection is not the issue so much as coherence among words, values, and actions. Do people see us doing what we say we are going to do?

For a number of years, a United Methodist pastor served in Mississippi with great difficulty. He and his family moved regularly from one modest pastorate to another, sometimes after only one year. The reasons for the frequent moves were many. The educational, personal, and social differences between pastor and assigned congregations were gigantic. Nevertheless, near the surface of parish conflict with their pastor was a profound witness by the pastor against the segregation and racism of the day.

When the United States Supreme Court rendered a decision in late 1969 that finally instituted unitary school systems across the South, this pastor was serving a white

31

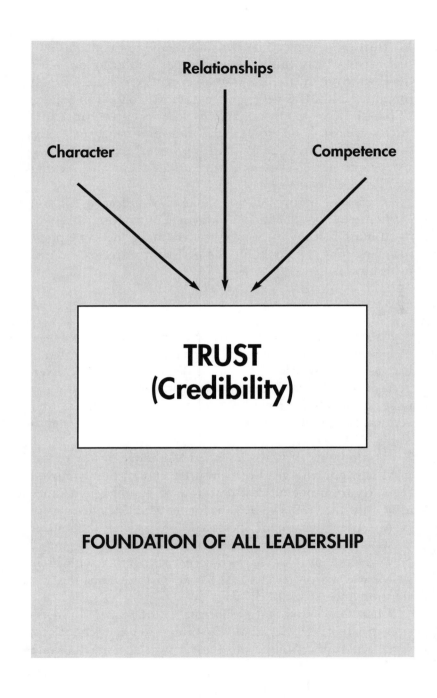

congregation in the Mississippi Delta where pronounced African American population majorities are common. The pastor's community was in a school district affected by the ruling. Within a matter of weeks, whites left the public school system, with the exception of the pastor's children.

A committee from the church made an appointment with the United Methodist bishop to talk about their pastoral appointment for the coming year. Bishops were accustomed to meeting with delegations upset with this particular pastor. Nevertheless, the bishop was surprised by the delegation's message. They said, "We don't agree or understand what our pastor and his family are doing. However, we respect his commitment to his beliefs. We understand, Bishop, that it may be best for our pastor's family to move. But, we want you to know that our request to you is that our pastor whom we respect be returned for another year."

Personal leadership and organizational leadership require the persistent example and power of character and integrity. A study of exemplary leaders among Catholic health systems found a profound synthesis of values and actions.[10] Integrity strengthens the capabilities of leaders and institutions to address pressing needs. As Rosita de Ann Mathews puts it, "Integrity builds structures that become impervious to demonic penetration."[11]

Trust that comes from the character of the leader accumulates over countless personal and public encounters where the leader behaves in a way that communicates honesty and integrity. Each experience can contribute to the credibility a leader needs for maximum effectiveness. Although the effects are quite practical for a leader, the motivation is far from calculating. Leaders of character behave in honorable ways because of who they are and who they seek to become as children of God and leaders called by God for leadership on behalf of the entire community of faith.

In this sense, the character of the leader can never be separated from the calling of the leader. Although *calling* is often associated only with a calling to ordained ministry, here the term is used more broadly to refer to that claim that God has placed on all of our lives for service. We must be connected to our calling from God. Jesus taught as one having authority, and not as the scribes. The scribes had positional authority, but that did not mean they had the authority that comes from an inner conviction of God's calling. Our calling from God represents the essence of our spiritual identity. It is who we are before God. It embodies our mission in life. While we continue to seek greater clarity about God's call on our lives, we will always take with us into any setting the call of God that claims and guides our lives.

Christian leaders must see all leadership rooted in what God has called them to be and do. But more is needed. If we were to be spiritual entrepreneurs or private practitioners, then our own conviction might be sufficient. But Christian leaders always function within a community of faith. A key part of that legitimizing comes from the larger community of faith that not only confirms our call from God but also calls us to various roles of leadership. These "assignments," as Jürgen Moltmann refers to them, are to be fulfilled on behalf of the whole church. The leadership roles never become private possessions to be guarded and protected. Leadership is about service, not prerogative.

Competence

A third imperative for trust is competence. If Christian leaders operate from callings from God and the church, there is a sense in which there is a third calling that comes from the context of a leader's service. Leadership is finally about real people in actual circumstances. Paul speaks of authority being used for "building up" and not for "tearing down." People may give us a leadership position, but the authority needed to lead must be worked out among the people with whom we serve and the actual circumstances they face at a particular time.

Can constituents depend on the leader's faithfulness in accomplishing what they have a right to expect from their leaders? Are leaders servants of the vision of the group? People may have warm feelings for a leader, but if they are consistently disappointed in the leader's accomplishment of basic expectations, trust will soon evaporate. People may trust the honesty of a leader, but if the leader is not addressing effectively the current needs, trust will not remain strong.

A study of outstanding leaders in nonprofit organizations found that professional competence was essential to their success.[12] Likewise, a study of very large congregations found that their pastoral leaders "establish their authority or right to lead not primarily by virtue of the office they hold or because of their formal credentials, but more by a combination of *demonstrated competence* and *religious authenticity.*"[13]

There is obviously a technical dimension to competence. Leaders must be grounded in basic knowledge and skills related to their leadership role. For clergy this must include those disciplines associated with theological education. Without biblical, theological, historical, and professional knowledge and skills adequate to the pastor's situation, successful leadership is severely jeopardized. Clearly for every leadership position there is some baseline educational competence required, though even the most educated and gifted of God's leaders must always remember that our ultimate "competence is from God, who has made us competent to be ministers of a new covenant" (2 Cor. 3:5-6).

Although a degree of technical competence is essential, note that the competence most required is not competence of a type that might be judged and ranked by tests. Rather, the need is for applied competence that assesses what is most needed for a particular time and place and a willingness to assume responsibility for leading people to move in appropriate directions. "Stewardship begins," according to Peter Block, "with the willingness to be accountable for some larger body than ourselves—an organization, a community . . . It requires a level of trust that we are not used to holding."[14]

Leaders are willing to do what is required, to accept responsibility for faithfulness to mission, to pursue an appropriate vision, and to maintain the healthy functioning of the group. Such leaders guide groups in making decisions to enhance mission, and to admit mistakes and change direction when necessary.

Everyone suffers when leaders never get seriously focused on what is most needed by the group and never see themselves as accountable to the group or for the results of the group. Warren Carter captures this sense of appropriate action in the New Testament when he talks about action (doing something) and mission (a community sent out) as constitutive of early church leadership. Competence illustrates that personal authenticity is not enough. Authenticity and fitting action must come together. Being and doing cannot be separated in understanding trustworthy leadership.

When I was in high school, our football team went two years with only one win. To make matters worse, this dry spell came after many years of superior teams under the leadership of a coach who had left. My father was a member of the school board when the superintendent recommended, after the second failed season, that the current football coach be dismissed. The board members knew a change was needed, but firing someone is never easy. One board member who attended the same church as the coach said, "I hate to see us let him go because he is such a good man." Bringing a sense of reality back to the group, another school board member replied, "My mother was a good woman. But she was no football coach." The board made a coaching change.

Leaders should always be concerned with the question, "What should I be as a person?" They must also keep before them the other question, "What should I be doing?"

Garry Wills maintains that most leadership literature is

unitarian when it should be trinitarian. (And he is not speaking theologically!) "Unitarian" leadership focuses on the leader. "Trinitarian" leadership has the leader as the "one who mobilizes others toward a goal shared by the leader and followers. . . . Leaders, followers, and goals make up the three equally necessary supports for leadership."[15]

Leaders come to be seen not as persons pursuing their own agendas but, in the words of Robert Greenleaf, as servants of a vision and always seeking a better one. Such leaders keep pointing everyone toward the overall mission and calling, all to find their place in the fulfillment of a mission far greater and grander than any individual.

TRUST BECOMES LEADERSHIP THROUGH AN INSPIRING VISION

If trust consists of relationships, character, and competence, then inspiration is the ingredient that transforms such trust into effective and compelling leadership. There must be something that distinguishes leadership from mere moral and competent management. Great leaders exude energy and passion for a cause greater than themselves.

Warren Carter speaks of leadership in the New Testament representing an alternative community to the conventional wisdom of its society. Christian community was not the same as the world around them. This was not a separatist model. Indeed, Christians lived in the cities and used language and cultural symbols of their time. They were also different. Their commitment to a vision larger than that of the world made all the difference in their lives.

Such leaders lift up the "not yet" of God's preferred future and inspire others to make the sometimes difficult journey to the fulfillment of the alternative vision. Leaders do more than manage the circumstances they inherit. They understand that leadership is about pointing to that "land that never has been," in the words of Langston Hughes.

Descartes understood what finally motivates humans. "The passions are the only advocates," he said, "that always persuade." Such passion does not come so much from a leader eliminating all the difficulties faced by people. Indeed, both biblical and secular history remind us that passion comes from a deep and abiding belief that one is a part of something truly important, despite the sacrifices and suffering that often accompany such a journey.

It is to that journey toward a congregation's "not yet" that we now turn in the remainder of the book. Many suggestions will be offered for discerning the next faithful chapter in a church's unfolding story. Effective leaders resist the temptation to get preoccupied with the specifics of strategies and techniques. They always remember that visioning is spiritual discernment over which we finally have no control. They also remember that the greatest asset one can bring to congregational renewal leadership is the bond of trust established with others in the church. Building such trust is hard work, and it takes time. However, it is, as Peg C. Neuhauser has put it, the "cultural foundation stone" on which everything else rests.[16]

Chapter 2
Define Your Congregation's Reality

The beginning of wisdom is to call things by their right names.

Chinese proverb

One of the first responsibilities of any leader is to help define the reality the group is facing.

Defining reality is not the same thing as naming reality to fit one's own agenda or priorities. It will involve making assessments and judgments, but leaders make every effort to name the character of the reality rather than a version of reality that fits their own interests. Leaders seek to say as accurately as possible, "This is what we are facing together."

Nothing is more limiting to a group than the inability to talk about the truth.

Peter Senge[1]

OBLIVIOUS TO REALITY

Over time, groups can become oblivious to reality. Sometimes they work hard at shielding themselves from it. Careful stories and rationalizations are often developed to pretend reality is otherwise. Some have described this process as the "collective suppression of countervailing evidence." Such denial of reality is found to a greater or lesser degree in most organizations. It is said that the British War

Office kept three sets of figures about casualties in World War I—"one to mislead the public, another to mislead the Cabinet, and the third to mislead itself."[2]

Lyle Schaller contends that the majority of North American Protestant congregations founded before 1970 are in a "state of denial." After giving examples of contemporary denial (such as, "the refusal to believe that most of the people born after 1955 bring a different set of expectations to church than are carried by those born before 1940"), he goes on to give clues about how denial might most effectively be handled through a process of helping define reality. He suggests that, after recognizing that denial is never a source of creativity, one should "flood the system with accurate information describing contemporary reality."[3] Only then can necessary solutions emerge.

It is not unlike walking out of one's house and suddenly noticing something in the grass. Mary Parker Follett tells of such a dilemma in which one person in a group may look ahead and see a "snake" while another in the group sees a "fallen branch." The key leadership task at that moment is to define the reality correctly. Whether the object is a snake or a fallen branch makes a tremendous difference in determining what action is needed.

Systems are notoriously adept at colluding around answers that will not make a difference. Congregations faced with an obvious need for change in what they are doing in ministry . . . will sometimes remain in a state of denial and may even find a way to talk about how their future will be better, even though they do not plan to change what they are doing.

Gil Rendle[4]

The key question at such a time is not who should make the decision about the process of decision making. Having the decision made by the person with the positional "leadership" of the group or by the group member with the highest education, or by the person who paid for the excursion will be of scant comfort if an incorrect judgment is made. Likewise, having the decision made through a process of total group participation, by a process assuring "ownership" of the decision by the group, or by simply voting will bring no satisfaction if the process, wonderful as it may be, does not render a proper assessment of the reality faced by the group.

The key question is, "What is the nature of the situation in which we find ourselves?" Anything less is inadequate as a basis for next steps. Once there is a correct definition of reality, then, and only then, can planning begin regarding appropriate next actions.

The "snake or branch" illustration above is a classic example of both the importance of defining reality and its limitations. Follett points out accurately that once a group decides that what lies before them is actually a snake, the next steps are not obvious. There very well may not be automatic agreement about what to do with this information. Different people may respond quite differently to the presence of the snake. There is still work to be done to ascertain the appropriate leadership responses to the reality that we now all agree exists.

Defining reality properly gives a basis for substantive difference. Difference based on ignorance or inaccuracy is meaningless. "We have not done away with difference," Follett contends, "but we have provided the possibility for fruitful difference." The goal is not to do away with difference, including differing interpretations of the same facts. The goal, according to Follett, is to do away with "*muddle*."[5]

We do well to remember the words of the poet Wallace

Stevens that we live in our description of a place and not in the place itself. Leaders have as a first task the clear and honest "description of a place" that permits leadership to take place. The "place itself" will not generate needed change without such fitting descriptive work.

PROPHETIC DESCRIPTION BEFORE PRESCRIPTION

Such description, reinterpretation, framing, and reframing is precisely what spiritual leaders do all the time. The proclamation of God's reign is meaningless unless framed within the realities present at a particular time. Some would contend that the truth of Christian faith is not as much about "oughts" as it is about defining the reality of God, the world, humanity, and the relationship of God with the world and its people. Parker Palmer says that "spiritual traditions are an effort to penetrate the illusions of the external world and to name its underlying truth."[6]

Unhappy is a people that has run out of words to describe what is going on.
Thurman Arnold

Is this not what the preacher is about in every sermon? The preacher holds up the realities of our lives and the reality of God's eternal truth in such a way that hearers are able to see themselves and their futures in new and redemptive ways. What may appear as descriptive becomes liberating as we come to see God's new possibilities for the future. "Before the gospel is good news," says Frederick Buechner, "it is simply the news that that's the way it is."[7]

This is what Nehemiah did. After careful listening, inspection of the situation, and prayer, Nehemiah said, "You see the trouble we are in." It was only when the ruin of

Jerusalem with its burned gates was named that the appropriate vision—"Come, let us rebuild the wall"—could emerge as a common effort. With a shared understanding of the reality, it was possible for the people to commit "themselves to the common good" (Neh. 2).

So it was with many biblical prophets. They were able to lift up a description of temporal and spiritual realities that called people to the change and the redemption God makes possible. The same can be said of Jesus. His words can be seen as exhortations, but they can also be seen as descriptions of the way life is when lived in communion with God or outside God's will. Before many sayings are prescriptions for behavior, they are descriptions of life. The Beatitudes are an example. They declare "Blessed (or happy) *are* the merciful, for they will receive mercy" or "Blessed *are* the pure in heart, for they will see God" (Matt. 5:7-8, italics added).

In more recent times, Martin Luther King, Jr., exercised prophetic leadership by describing the reality of racial injustice in compelling and memorable ways. It was only as people came to see the massive oppression of African Americans that change was possible. King, in the spirit of prophets of old and all effective leaders today, went beyond description to define a dream of God's preferred future. Nevertheless, the dream only took on meaning when put side-by-side with an honest portrayal of reality.[8]

As we will see, all leadership comes from holding in tension the true current reality with a compelling and energizing vision for the future. Leadership comes, according to Peter Senge, when "people articulate a vision and tell the truth (to the best of their ability) about current reality." Richard Parrott puts this well for church leaders, "Speak the truth about the current situation and articulate a vision that energizes people. Anyone in the church who does that is a leader."

DIFFERING VIEWS OF REALITY

What if others do not agree with the description of reality that emerges? That sometimes happens. If so, the discussion that follows need not be a personal struggle or a political debate. Instead, leaders invite from everyone new information others consider more accurate. If everyone knows that their leaders, while having particular interests, want most to describe the common situation, then no one need be threatened.

If a reality emerges of an "increasingly older congregation," someone may disagree saying, "I see lots of young people at church." Leaders may respond by saying, "Perhaps you are right. How might we determine most accurately if the average age of our congregation has been going up or down over the past ten years?" Without a well-defined reality, people spend their efforts in utterly unprofitable directions. If everyone is working from the assumption that "there are lots of young people," and the reality is that the church has been getting sharply older for years, then no amount of hard work, prayer, or faithfulness will make much difference. It is amazing how people often make decisions and plan for the future out of faulty assumptions and mythology. An effort to define reality will help in seeing which assumptions are based on fact and which are not.

Myths are tempting assumptions about congregational life. Just as cheese lures a mouse, myths lure us to beliefs we want to be true. . . . Myths allow us to avoid change. Myths permit us to use the same old methods to get the same old results. Myths immobilize and trap us in dead ends, blocking us from fully living out the answer to our most important question: What is God calling us to be and do as a congregation?

Cynthia Woolever and Deborah Bruce[9]

An experience in a local church illustrates the point well. All the talk among church members was that a new youth worker was needed to bring the church back to a day remembered from the past when the church was "filled with youth." The pastor could have responded as a manager, setting out to arrange for a search in response to the hope for revived youth ministry. Instead, the pastor responded as a leader. Although equally concerned about youth ministry, the pastor instead led the governing board in a study of some relevant data. In the process they discovered that the church actually had a higher percentage of the youth of the community in the current youth ministry than at the "heyday" of the church years before. This insight came as they compared church statistics with community population information.

In the process they also discovered that their community has one of the highest adult illiteracy rates in the state. This was a surprising revelation to a congregation in which there is no adult illiteracy. This new picture of reality helped them make plans better suited to their current mission calling. Ministry fitting of God's call upon them at this time and place is more probable under these circumstances. Renewed vitality and strengthened discipleship are now far more likely. With a large number of educators in the congregation and more than adequate physical space, this church was ideally positioned to lead an ecumenical community effort of awareness and action about adult illiteracy.

SEEING THE WHOLE PICTURE

The task of defining reality may sound simple, but it is far from that. "Reality" may not even be the right word.

45

"Realities" is perhaps the more accurate term. There are always many different realities influencing the life of the church or any other group. This is a reason always to have different people around the discussion table who understand the various realities facing the congregation but, at the same time, can exercise judgment and selectivity regarding those realities that are most relevant and pressing currently.

The United Negro College Fund (UNCF) published a reference book that compiled decades of information on African Americans and higher education. The need for this data book was conceived by the president of UNCF, William H. Gray III, who formerly served for many years in Congress. Gray, who also serves as pastor of a large congregation in Philadelphia, wrote of the need for accurate information: "When I was in Congress, I saw that much of our educational policy was based on what I call knothole scholarship," he said. "If you try to watch a baseball game through a knothole, you have to guess about what you're missing—and you miss a lot." Gray also observed that "we exploded some myths" through the collection of data.

Defining realities and "exploding myths" are foundational for faithful ministry. What are the key realities that will influence vibrant witness for God? What realities give us clues for what God is calling us to do in the immediate future? What changes are taking place? What is new? What is different? What are the living edges today? What are the dying edges? Where are signs of hope? Where is conventional wisdom right? Where do conventional assumptions not match facts?

"Defining" reality may also connote a much too one-dimensional process. The leader may never "define" reality as a carefully-thought-through and presented analysis. Instead, the process is more likely to be helping people "discover" the reality in which they live. Insights discov-

46

ered have much more power for people than information merely heard. The leader must always keep in mind the purpose here. It is not to win a debate. The goal is for people to have a common and reasonably accurate understanding of reality out of which decisions and actions can emerge.

Many find it helpful to collect the reliable information in a concise manner. The leader then asks many individuals and small groups to study the material and report the most important clues and insights for planning for the future. The important thing here is that people are working with the same trusted information. Collecting and using such information will be a key component of the visioning process outlined later in the book.

In one local church a comment heard often in recent years was, "We need more space." Constant problems with scheduling programs and meetings kept this "need" on everyone's mind. The trustees had tried for years to acquire more land for a building expansion, but without success.

A new trustee chair asked the pastor, staff, and others to help the trustees collect space information about their church and other churches of comparable size and program. The church actually discovered that they had more square feet of building space than any of the other churches they consulted, including some significantly larger in membership. The "reality" they discovered was not a space shortage but issues of space utilization, design, and condition. Now the trustees could give up their futile efforts to secure more space and turn immediately to what was needed—reshaping existing space, making more space accessible, and renovating space that was not in use currently because of its condition. These changes, along with a better system for scheduling and assigning activities to available and appropriately sized rooms, met all the space needs for the congregation's ministry.

USING QUESTIONS FOR INSIGHT, NOT BLAME

Leaders must help define reality carefully, or they never get beyond step one of leading change. Using key questions is preferable to providing solutions. Leaders do not have to have the answers. Leaders must have the right questions. It is these right questions that open the doors to new discoveries that may provide a foundation for change.

A pastor went to a new church with a long history and much tradition. It was a prestigious assignment for this pastor. Much was new, including some of the terminology. For the first time ever, the pastor heard church members say, "Preacher, we don't have any money problems." Talk about a new experience!

The new pastor could have found ways to enjoy and benefit from this newfound financial security. Instead, the pastor showed appreciation for the resources of the congregation but, at the same time, found ways to begin using probing questions with lay leaders of the congregation. Some of the questions used were: Who's missing in this congregation? Where are we vulnerable as a congregation? If current trends continue, what will our church look like in ten years?

What the pastor and laity discovered was that their ample financial resources, despite decades of membership loss, were made possible by an aging, loyal, and financially well-to-do constituency. Their membership above the age of fifty-five was as strong as churches with much larger total memberships. People, as a rule, tend to have more assets at that age than at any other time in their lives. That was why fewer people did not lead immediately to congregational financial stress.

They also discovered that below the age of fifty-five, there were few members indeed. Out of this assessment of reality, a new vision for the church emerged focused on children.

There were few children in the church; but their surveys showed that there were many children (and their parents) in the community who were "missing" from this congregation, and the congregation had many resources for children's ministry, if so deployed. The new vision became a reality. As it turned out, the older members, who were the ones required later to build the new buildings for the expanding children's ministry, were some of the most enthusiastic supporters of the new vision. They could now see a future for their church.

"Show Me the Evidence"

(A pastor who went to a 100-year-old church in serious twenty-year decline tells a story of renewal.)

Before going to this church eight years ago, I heard tragic stories about the church. Most of the members were dead or dying, I was told, except for the mean ones who are alive and well! Needless to say, I went reluctantly, but leading this church has been one of the greatest experiences of my life.

It was here that I began, out of necessity, my personal quest in leadership. Everyone knew something was wrong, yet nothing changed. I began with a positive attitude. I was consumed with a passion for renewal. Average attendance was 56, and the average age over 65. With no children or programs, members feared the church would close.

We formed a vision team, did enormous research, and prayed. We met weekly. Our findings were clear. The church was a numerical nightmare, and the spirit was gone. Nevertheless, the demographics also revealed that things could be different. The community was actually growing as our church was dying. What was wrong?

We found we had generational, organizational, and spiritual issues keeping us from growing. A

49

turning point came when we stopped looking for what was "most" wrong. Two persons from different generations attacked each other personally. "We are not about finding fault but getting better," I said. "Let's just deal with the evidence." A breakthrough occurred. Now we were looking for solutions.

We did not worry about things we could *not* do. We sought to change the things that we could. We changed our organization, developed a mission statement, and trained leadership. We celebrated and dreamed big dreams. Our goals were achievable and measurable. My key contribution was in bringing a diverse group together, helping them understand the facts, and, therefore, change the future.

Today our average attendance is 165 with an average age of 41. We have relevant worship, small group Bible study, fellowship activities, and active missions. We plan to relocate to a new site more adequate for our expanding ministry.

Many people need to be involved in the process of defining reality. Different eyes will spot different things. It will be vitally important to look for what discoveries tend to be made repeatedly by different people and groups looking at the same material. The process is not about "ownership"— as crucial as that is—but about discernment. Many people must be engaged not because of political considerations but because this is a spiritual discernment task. Many people are required because no one of us has all of God's wisdom, but every one of us will have a part of the needed wisdom. Knowing the power of description, we should always approach the task with great care and with a genuine openness to what God will reveal to us.

Although leaders must assure that reality is being

assessed, it is important for the conclusions to arise from the shared deliberations of many others. A leader prematurely announcing the reality may mean that the leader's interpretation of the situation remains the leader's alone and never reaches the broad consensus required for action. Particularly when the reality contains bad news, as it often does, it is best for those George Thompson describes as "culture bearers" to deliver the bad news. Thompson is referring particularly to information that questions the assumption of survivability, but the advice applies broadly to conclusions that may question the more optimistic assumptions of the congregation.

Culture bearers are longtime members who have the trust of the membership and who know the congregation well, including "where the land mines are." Since these culture bearers are heavily invested in church, "they have the capital to risk triggering an explosion." Thompson illustrates with Esther, a church member who " 'got away with' telling the bishop, in front of her fellow parishioners, that their parish was dead." She could do so because of her place within the church family.[10]

Clergy, and newer lay leadership, will generally not have the store of cultural capital to tell congregations what is wrong with them and how they need to change. Such leaders must assure that the conditions and processes exist for trusted information to be examined broadly, for insights and clues for the future to emerge from all quarters, and for trusted culture bearers to be in a position both to understand the lay of the land and to serve as some key interpreters of the situation they are in.[11]

A well-defined reality is just the beginning of the larger task of leadership. Reality never turns out to be quite as simple as are our somewhat-informed preconceptions, stereotypes, and analyses. Reality can be utterly disconcerting sometimes. Perceptive leaders should always be on the lookout for the disquieting evidence. Life is simpler if one can avoid being confused with the facts. The other side is that understanding reality helps everyone know what is being faced. One can feel fairly confident that energy is going toward what the pressing needs are.

REFRAMING

Reframing is an important method of defining (or redefining) reality. Leaders find ways to reframe issues in order to clarify the values and competing interests that always surround various understandings of reality. Within all groups, people have their own interests and values. Generally, those interests and values are not bad, but they are too limiting if not put in some larger context. Without help, people will look at everything through the lens of their own values and immediate interests and miss much else—instead of looking at their own interests in light of a larger vision.

Effective leaders find ways to acknowledge those often-competing values in a way that permits people to see their own particular interests in light of a larger vision. The issues facing a congregation need to be reframed around larger values while not ignoring or devaluing the more narrow interests. This is what O'Toole calls the "creation of moral symmetry among those with competing values."[12]

Church members of various ages and circumstances share interests that may seem urgent only to them. Generational cohorts normally share certain perspectives. Parents of preschool children will have particular concerns. Homebound members have special interests. Youth bring their interests. People especially attached to individual program emphases of the congregation will tend to see things from these perspectives. Paid staffs have interests. On and on the list could go.

If the tasks of framing and reframing are not being done in an active manner, the leader is left always to respond to the different interests that are competing for priority. This is a sure prescription for making a manager out of a leader.

Managers do the work that must be done, but may have no vision beyond just what people want. Leaders are always seeking and pursing a vision guided by compelling values. Leaders are managers, but leaders are much more than managers. Without taking the initiative to put smaller goals into a larger vision, a leader will spend inordinate time trying to satisfy the various limited interests and resolve conflicts among competing claims without these efforts contributing necessarily to any larger aim.

Adam Hamilton, pastor of the United Methodist Church of the Resurrection in Leawood, Kansas, does reframing as well as anyone I have ever known.[13] The Church of the Resurrection began with a small group meeting in a mortuary. Later the church moved to the gymnasium of an elementary school. Then the first worship space of their own was built (which now serves as the narthex for the current sanctuary). This congregation now averages 6,000 in attendance at worship with six worship services every weekend.

One can imagine the challenges of dealing with such phenomenal growth. In addition to providing space and leadership for such large numbers, Adam faced the everyday challenge of leading a congregation that looked one way when people first joined and now looks quite different in size and outreach. Although there is excitement in the rapid growth, there is also a sense of loss by some, particularly those who remember when the church consisted of only a few dozen or a few hundred people.

Adam has found numerous ways to reframe the interests of those feeling loss—ways that incorporate their values into a larger vision. For example, on one occasion Adam reported a conversation in which a church member asked, "How big are we going to get?" in a tone that indicated the questioner felt the church was already too large. Adam's reply to the inquirer was that he did not know since there were clearly more "nonreligious and nominally religious" persons in the community, those who have been at the heart of the church's mission from the beginning.

Adam then used this as the occasion to say that he sometimes shares the sentiments of those who long for the earlier days when the church was smaller. "It was wonderful when I was able to know every member by name, to visit every new visitor, and to be involved in every event at the church. I miss those experiences a lot." "However," he continued, "when I catch myself focusing too much on those days, I remember that we are called to be more than a *Cheers* church "where everybody knows your name," referring to the theme song from the popular television program]. God has something more in mind for our church. I still miss knowing everyone well, but I celebrate the opportunity to be a part of a great movement of God in this community."

Instead of devaluing the feelings of a portion of the congregation, he acknowledged their normal feelings and then reframed them to become a part of a much larger vision for the church. In a sense, by identifying with their emotions, he gave them the chance they needed to join him in understanding the feelings and *at the same time* join others in the larger effort.

"Do We Really Need This Much More Space?"

Facing a $30 million capital campaign for the next phase of expansion for the Church of the Resurrection, pastor Adam Hamilton could hear rumblings questioning if this much space were necessary. "With the building projects we have already completed," they asked, "don't we have more space than other churches already?"

Adam did his research and then helped reframe the discussion in order to put the space concerns in a different perspective. Acknowledging that some had asked the legitimate question about the need for such a large amount of additional space, he reported on research he had done to make sure the church's projected plans were reasonable. First, he told about some churches in different parts of the country comparable to Church of the Resurrection in worship attendance. Adam had visited many of them during a summer sabbatical a few years before. He reported that these churches have between fifty and ninety square feet of building space per average worshiper. Next Adam turned to churches in the local area with which the congregation would be more familiar. They also, it turned out, have between fifty and ninety square feet per average worshiper.

Church of the Resurrection at the time had fifteen square feet of building space per worshiper. Using a visual to make his point in a memorable way, Adam brought out a piece of poster board fifteen square feet in size. Reminding everyone that this small space represented not only their individual physical space but also included hallways, restrooms, and other public areas beyond the actual space they occupy within the sanctuary. The point was made, and the space issue was put in a relevant perspective.

INTERVENTION OPTIONS FOR LEADERS

Ronald A. Heifetz and Marty Linsky offer four types of interventions that leaders may find useful in helping congregations define reality: observations, questions, interpretations, and actions.[14]

Observations. Here one reflects back to a group what the current situation appears to be or what one senses the group is saying or doing. No judgment or evaluation is involved.

Questions. This is perhaps the greatest tool for leaders. "What does all this mean?" "What do you think is going on here?" "Why do you think this is the case?" "How do you explain what we have discovered?"

Interpretations. There is a place for interpretations but not too soon. A leader may have had an insight for quite some time, but wanted to give time for more information to come in and to see how others came to view the situation. If it is clear that the leader has thought about the issues carefully and has reasons for a particular interpretation, people are generally quite open to hearing that "take" on things. The leader will need to be prepared for this interpretation to be questioned and perhaps refined by the insights of others. The point is not to win an argument; a leader is trying to help a group discern the true state of things.

Actions. One can see that with each of these interventions the stakes become higher. Action calls attention, and any action is susceptible to more than one interpretation. That is why Heifetz and Linsky insist that the message and context of any action be "crystal clear."

A pastor may decide to have a Youth Sunday in order to communicate support for the emerging consensus within the church that youth ministry is an area of great vulnerability and possibility in the coming years. The pastor thinks that a youth-planned and youth-led worship service will send just the right signal to the youth, to the parents of the youth, and to those working especially hard on the visioning committee. However, the congregation may see the music the youth use throughout the service as the pastor's way of weighing in on a simmering conflict among the worship committee, music committee, and music staff around the traditional versus contemporary worship debate. The ensuing misunderstanding could take precious energy and time away from what, until that time, was a growing consensus for a vision focusing on youth ministry.

Defining reality may be done in a variety of ways and requires the wisdom of many people. Whatever the approach, it is the responsibility of the leader to see that it is done—and done carefully and accurately.

Chapter 3
Discern a Vision

Where there is no vision, the people perish.
Proverbs 29:18, KJV

It is important to discover a vision that fits your church and addresses its realities. All organizations, including churches, face a dilemma. Every organization rests on a cultural foundation of shared assumptions, values, and practices. This is the glue that holds a group together over time. Without such ties, a group would disintegrate after one gathering. While necessary for a group's existence, this cultural foundation also can be a prime source of resistance to change.

Thus, a church's culture—who we are and how we do things around here—is both essential and a source of great resistance. But it cannot be ignored. Culture and values lead to resistance and, at the same time, provide the basis for any lasting change. Only the culture can hold the group together during the change process and sustain the change into the future.

Therefore, it is never enough to be "right" in the sense of knowing technically what the church should do. For example, it is not enough to know how much parking is needed, how many worship services are needed, what type of worship is needed, where the church should relocate, and so forth. Leaders must find ways for any proposed change to be right for the particular church's culture. Only this type of applied wisdom will lead to beneficial change.

If the leader ignores the need to be attentive to the church's culture, the leader runs the risk of destroying the very culture and cohesion needed to sustain the new vision. Leaders have to work hard at preserving the continuity of strong cultural values at the same time that efforts for change are taking place. In fact, the more change that is taking place, the more a church will need to focus on its common, shared values.

There are no clean slates in established organizations, including churches. The artistic effect called "pentimento" comes to mind. Lillian Hellman, in a book by this name, describes the effect. "Old paint on canvas, as it ages, sometimes becomes transparent. When that happens it is possible, in some pictures, to see original lines: a tree will show through a woman's dress, a child makes way for a dog, a large boat is no longer on the open sea."[1] So it is in the life of every congregation.

Willie Morris illustrates this concept by remembering that, until recently, on the Hinds County Courthouse restroom door bearing the sign "Women," one could make out beneath the coat of paint the words "Colored Women." A heritage, for good or bad, is always there showing through. The past showing through can be changed, but the heritage cannot be ignored. Morris goes on to illustrate such a change when he points out that in the same building in Mississippi "where secession was approved in 1860 there now stands a prominent and permanent exhibit on the civil rights movement."[2]

"Every leader, to be effective," said Alfred North Whitehead, "must simultaneously adhere to the symbols of change and revision and the symbols of tradition and stability."[3] Leaders have to work hard at preserving the continuity of strong cultural values at the same time that efforts for change are taking place.

Because cultures, like personalities of individuals, take a long time to develop and a long time to change, one can normally achieve better results by using an existing culture, good or bad, rather than by trying to destroy an old culture and build a new one. It is not likely that one will be able to destroy a culture and then rebuild another one strong enough to carry a vision in the time most people are in leadership positions.

WHAT IS CULTURE?

Culture is the shape a place takes when it's inside the head of its peoples—all the habits, attitudes and values they take for granted.

Fintan O'Toole[4]

Culture is in essence "who we are and how we do things around here." It captures all the spoken and unspoken assumptions that make up a particular community of faith. A congregation's culture will share countless similarities with that of other churches, but the way those elements are expressed and especially how they are combined makes each culture unique.

George Thompson refers to culture as "shared meaning and behavior" and has done an excellent job of delineating some of the various cultural streams that come together to make a congregation's culture. The most obvious and easiest to identify are a church's cultural *artifacts*. Such things as the type of hymnal in the pews, where the pulpit is located, and an American flag in the sanctuary are examples of artifacts. What can be confusing is that artifacts do not necessarily mean the same thing in each congregation. The second level of culture Thompson names is *espoused values*. "We are a friendly church" is an example. Again, espoused values appear obvious, but the meaning behind what is said is not self-evident. The third level is *shared basic assumptions*.

These are the most important but the hardest to uncover. They are so taken for granted that there is no reason to name them. Newcomers, clergy or lay, normally discover these foundational assumptions by violating one. Thompson refers to that as stepping on a land mine.[5]

Thompson also names some useful layers of culture that help one to understand the components of a congregation's culture. "Congregations live in culture they create, but they don't create culture out of nothing," Thompson notes. "There are various layers in the church's context, each one functioning as a 'host' from which the church unquestioningly draws."[6]

Macroculture is the broad cultural context in which a church functions. Churches in the United States, for example, operate within a particular national cultural context of stories, history, and symbols.

Mesoculture, or middle layers of culture, sometimes have a more powerful shaping influence on congregational culture. Some of these layers that Thompson names that come together in various combinations within churches are:

Regional
Racial/ethnic
Class
Traditional Orality
Generational

Then there is *Microculture*. Every local setting and congregation has its own peculiarities and practices. This is the idiosyncratic nature of particular local cultures. Sometimes these are challenging to understand, especially why things are done that way, but these things that appear as eccentricities are as real and important in that community as the most established practices of nations.[7]

While these various elements can be divided for discussion, they come as a uniquely woven fabric with a given congregation. When you walk into a congregation, you are entering "a stream of culture that is created out of many other streams," says Thompson. "It is the confluence of all the many idiosyncratic elements that meet in that one church in that certain way that makes each church distinctive."[8] It is tempting to ignore major aspects of a congregation's culture because their familiarity causes us to think we understand what they mean. Familiarity causes us to miss the rich diversity of cultural streams that the congregation embodies.

THE POWER OF ORGANIZATIONAL CULTURE

Any organization lives in the minds of its members. There may be organizational charts, bylaws, governing groups, annual reports; but the power of any congregation will be found in the hearts and minds of those who comprise the church. It is only as we are able to engage that deep and invisible cultural richness of meaning, beliefs, assumptions, symbols, and shared history that any attempt at change can stand a chance.

The role of organizational culture in change has received great emphasis recently. Culture is simply "how we do things around here." There are obvious artifacts of a culture (structures, policies, stories), but the most powerful cultural components are invisible. As we have seen, the strongest shared cultural assumptions are not discussed because they are taken for granted.

A leader quickly discovers "the way we do things here." Frequently this is a negative experience. A local church culture is often the first line of defense against change. This can cause leaders to react against the "local ways" and to try to change them. Leaders should be cautious in using personal preference to judge an organization's culture. Rather, the test of a culture should always be a missional one. Does the culture permit the church to fulfill its primary task?

Edgar H. Schein reminds us that culture is the "residue of

past successes."[9] Therefore, a leader should view the culture of an organization primarily as strengths upon which to build for the future. It is true that some of the culture will have become dysfunctional. But this portion is probably a small component of the overall picture, though it often tends to loom large, especially in the mind of new leaders. Our natural tendency is to see what is wrong immediately, while appreciating strengths can take longer.

Above all, leaders need always to have a good "cultural perspective" of their church or ministry setting. The result will be worth the effort. "Suddenly the world is much clearer," says Schein. "Anomalies are now explainable, conflicts are more understandable, resistance to change begins to look normal, and—most important—your own humility increases. In that humility, you will find wisdom."[10]

YOUR CONGREGATION'S STORY

Leaders today are familiar with the demand that they come forward with a new vision. But it is not a matter of fabricating a new vision out of whole cloth. A vision relevant for us today will build on values deeply embedded in human history and in our own tradition.

John W. Gardner[11]

R. Robert Cueni[12] stresses the importance of a church renewing out of its own distinctive culture and history. Cueni studied mainline congregations that were forty or more years old, "tall steeple," and that had renewed in recent years. He discovered that every one of them renewed out of their own distinct history and culture. They found a theme in their own story that most fit the current situation and used that theme as a bridge to their next chapter.

What Cueni describes from his study of large membership, older, mainline congregations is what can be seen in
churches of all types. Most existing congregations operate
out of histories that shape their futures just as our own backgrounds shape our futures. "Renewed communities change,"
Leander Keck says, "but rarely by lurching or by repudiat-
ing the identities formed by their histories."[13]

Lessons from Fifty Churches That Renewed
They worshiped, programmed, nurtured, and
organized for ministry and mission in a variety of
ways. Their ministers varied widely in theological
stance, leadership style, and personal demeanor.
Some congregations fit the definition of the high-
commitment church. Others make few demands on
their members. Some think of themselves as mission posts on the frontier of a post-Christian world.
Others operate on the assumption Christendom
still flourishes. . . .
[Yet] . . . a discernable pattern of shared characteristics emerged. . . . [I]t became obvious that
*renewal happened when intentional, high-expec-
tation leadership works within the congregation's
historical understanding—i.e. its story—to plan for
and sustain a vital faith community where mission
is clear and worship as well as program are indigenous to the life of the congregation.*[14]

The beginning of all visioning for the future is a thorough
understanding of both the importance and content of the
congregation's unique story. The way a church thinks about
and talks about itself, says Cueni, will "not only describe the
past and explain the way it organizes in the present, but also
determine the way it plans for change."[15] The leader learns
the story and keeps testing what part of that story will serve
the congregation well into the future. It is leadership that

works within the congregation's ongoing story of its faith journey that renews a congregation, not a generic program brought from another church where it worked, Cueni reminds us.

"A temptation that church leaders seem to face almost ceaselessly," says George Thompson, "is thinking about the future as basically a continuation of the past."[16] A new vision is not a redoing of what we have done in the past. The task is not one of repeating past success. Thompson suggests an exercise in "projecting heritage" as a means of "following meaning out of where it has been and into where it could be." The task is "applying lived meaning to the future."[17]

In the following story, a church discovered a deeply held and broadly shared value on which they could build for the future with unity and energy.

Rediscovering the Sunday School

A rural church of 200 members faced problems similar to those of many other churches around them. Attendance and membership had declined as many younger people left the community for jobs elsewhere. Each year brought financial struggles. Mission giving was down. Facilities were in poor repair and not used fully. Morale was low.

During some listening sessions sponsored by the church council to get ideas for how the church could renew, church leaders were surprised to hear the large number of references to the Sunday school. Why would people focus on the Sunday school when there had not been a children's or youth Sunday school for several years? There were still three adult classes. Leaders concluded that church members associated a past time of church strength with a strong Sunday school.

On this basis, the church developed a vision around "Teaching the Faith to a New Generation."

They settled on the Sunday school as the center-piece of the vision, not because they had a strong Sunday school, but because there was a common shared value around it. This meant that limited effort had to go into "selling" the vision. Instead, church members said, "It's about time."

For the next two years, virtually everything the church did was seen through the lens of the Sunday school. An ecumenical vacation church school was held for the first time since 1965. The church began sponsoring Scout troops. An after-school program was established at the church. The newly organized children and youth classes presented monthly church supper programs. The existing adult classes took on the renovation of the classrooms for the new classes.

After two years, the church had a full Sunday school program again. However, other things were also different after two years. Worship attendance was up, church membership was up, mission giving was up, morale was high, and the physical facilities were in better shape than in many years.

WHAT ABOUT THE BAD THINGS IN A CONGREGATION?

It is quite likely that some aspects of an established church's culture are dysfunctional. Time may render some values no longer relevant. A leader's initial tendency may be to focus on the negative elements and try to "correct" or eliminate them. Yet, an immediate negative reaction against local culture may not serve the leader well.

What do you do with those dysfunctional, perhaps even idolatrous, elements of a church that are so irritating? Cueni provides as good an answer as I have seen. You ignore them. They become less significant over time through neglect. In a similar vein, Schein suggests that the more likely route to progress is to determine to face the future building on the positive elements of the existing culture, and not to spend time on the areas of weakness.

When cultural elements do need to be questioned, the leader does so on missional and practical grounds. Is this part of our life helping us to fulfill our primary task or not? To the extent that it is moving us closer to our mission, it is good. To the extent that it is hindering our mission, it must be questioned. There are clearly those practices within congregations that do not represent the highest, or even a faithful, Christian witness. They must be addressed, but we do so "on the way" toward our overall mission. It is not as if we are determined to stop everything to deal with the problem. One can give serious attention to those few practices that strike at the heart of Christian witness without letting that struggle become by default the all-consuming vision of the congregation.

In the next story of visioning, a church's "bad thing" was the loss through the years of virtually all of its younger membership.

A Vision for Children

A county seat church of 600 members seemed to face none of the problems of the rural churches in their county. While membership had declined steadily for twenty years, the church was still strong. There were no financial problems, the facilities were in good shape, and a new building had just been completed.

However, one leader in the church asked the question, "Where are we vulnerable?" The question led to considerable discussion. The conclusion was that, while the church was strong with members age 55 and above, the church had modest membership and participation below that age, at least for a church of that size.

This church developed a vision around children, "God Loves All the Children." Everything they did was viewed through the lens of serving the children they had and reaching other children. The shared commitment to children in this church was evident by the way in which older members engaged with this vision as eagerly as did the parents of the children. The church's history with children was seen in the displays of photographs of large groups of children from each chapter in the church's long history.

The vision succeeded. After five years, the number of children in the church grew from 35 to over 100. Furthermore, the twenty-year membership decline ceased. Not only was the church growing again, in two recent years, the church had a net gain of 50 members each year. Mission involvement increased, youth ministry flourished, and new community ministries were developed.

FINDING A BRIDGE TO YOUR CONGREGATION'S NEXT CHAPTER

Almost all new visions cross old bridges.
Observation by layperson at workshop

The task of visioning is not to write a new story but to write a new chapter in the ongoing story of a congregation. The story must be known and kept before the congregation. The story must also be built upon for this next chapter. A congregation's story must also be connected with the larger story of faith so that people are able to see what they are about as something beyond the story of any one congregation.

There must be a bridge over which a congregation can cross from one chapter to the next. A bridge makes possible the passage from where we are to where we need to be. That bridge will come out of the congregation's culture and heritage. It may be an historical event, a deeply embedded value, or a traditional strength. Notice how the church in the next case study found in an historical event the bridge they needed for the journey into their future.

A Church for Those Who Don't Fit Anywhere Else

A Mennonite student tells of her community in which there are four Mennonite churches. At one time all four churches, as well as many other churches in the community, were much stronger than today. Demographic and economic changes had left many community institutions with challenging situations. In this context, her church began a visioning process.

They looked in their heritage for clues for addressing the challenges of the new day. This church had at least one distinctive element in its history. The first three Mennonite churches in the community were established by and for distinct ethnic groups. The fourth, her church, was established by the denomination for persons who were not a part of the other three ethnic groups. As time went by and they studied their mission and values as well as demographic and community information, something about the way the church had begun seemed quite familiar.

Finally, someone identified the key for their "new" vision. "We are the church for those who don't fit anywhere else," was how it was named. They came to see that the future would not be different if they only concerned themselves with "people like us." In fact, "That is not who we are," someone said, "We began for those who were different." All of a sudden, they looked at their community in a fresh way. Instead of wondering where there were more Mennonites, they started seeing the many "different" people of the community as "their" people. They now saw workers in the community who had come from other countries and had tremendous language and other needs in a new way. They saw in a new light younger people who did not "fit" in any of the existing churches.

This church might have seen this outreach to those who appeared different from their traditional constituents as "giving up" who they are to become something else. Instead, they were able to move forward into a world of change confident that they were "being more of what we have always been."

YOUR CONGREGATION'S NEXT GENERATION

I found that older renewed churches are more like the next generation of family than they are like a new species.

R. Robert Cueni

Whenever a new child is born into a family, there is great joy. At that moment all the hopes, dreams, and love of an extended family surround the new life. Part of the joy at the birth is that this new child represents the next generation of a family heritage. Our hopes for this baby are not merely to repeat the lives of past family members. We obviously do not anticipate that this new child will emulate the bad parts of the family tradition that all families have. No, at the moment of new life, a family wants this child to share a rich family heritage, but they also want this child to "advance the plot" of the family's story. The goal is for this child to have all the resources of heritage as a foundation, and to develop in distinctive and new ways.

So it is with a congregation. A congregation renews out of its heritage. The bridge to the next chapter will come from that heritage. It may be that in time the changes in the new chapter will cause the church to look different enough that casual observers may say, "This is a different church than it used to be." But no matter how many changes take place, there is no way for a careful observer ever to view this church and not see the DNA of the congregation's past.

A pastor tells of visiting the home of a church member who has just died. The member was a tall, large, imposing man in his eighties. The man's size and demeanor sometimes led people to stand back. Some found him a bit intimidating. While visiting with people at the home, the pastor noticed across the room a woman around sixty years of age. She was thin, petite. Her smiling face radiated welcome and warmth. The pastor had never met this woman; but as soon as he saw her, he knew that she was the daughter of the man who had just died. While it was obvious that this daughter was different from her father in countless ways, there was no way that anyone who knew her father could see the daughter and not see the father's DNA. So it is with successful next generations in churches.

The next vision example is from a church that rediscovered an important component of its story as the building block for their next generation of service.

Remembering a Mission Heritage

A retired person told his new pastor about moving to this small community fifty years ago. Their church was the largest church in the town at that time. Over the years other churches had relocated closer to a new highway, developed facilities for youth ministry, and become larger churches.

This layperson reflected the sadness of a congregation whose identity had changed because of the loss of status of their church. Many others offered the new pastor suggestions. However, the pastor recognized that a part of their history and identity as important as size was mission. As their relative size diminished, so had their involvement in mission. As they paid attention to the contemporary interest in hands-on mission work, a new vision emerged—not around the size of membership but the size of their "heart for others" through mission. Their vision became "The Church with a Heart for Others."

The vision "took" because it was intimately tied to who they knew themselves to be. One can hardly move around in the church building today because of how the space is used to capacity for various mission enterprises. The church again has prominence in the community. Everyone knows the church as the "mission church." They also have renewed children's and youth ministry and a growing membership.

BECOMING MORE OF WHAT YOU HAVE ALWAYS BEEN

Change is not becoming something we never have been before. It is becoming more of what we have been. The last thing people need to hear is: "You know what you have valued in the past, you know how we have done things here in the past, well, that is the past. Now we are going to become something we have never been before."

What needs to be communicated clearly and repeatedly is: "You know what we have believed in the past, you know what has been important to this congregation from the beginning, you know what guided those who came before us in this church—well, we are now going to be more of that. We are going to be faithful to the best of our heritage."

Notice how the church in the next case study found a way to link new edges of need with old centers of heritage.

Beginning an AIDS Ministry

In the early years of broad public awareness of the AIDS epidemic, some members of the social concerns committee of a church in a medium-size community were anxious for their church to respond in some positive manner. In those days, people were well aware of AIDS, but there seemed to be as much misinformation and fear as there was solid information and positive directions, especially in communities their size. Yet, it was obvious that AIDS was already touching their community and their church, even if no one acknowledged the fact or stepped forward to respond.

The chair of the committee, while sympathetic to the interest of the committee members, was also aware of how controversial such a new ministry might be in a congregation not known for innovative or nonconventional actions. The pastor was also apprehensive, though willing for the committee to move forward. Over several months, the committee chair reported briefly to the governing council of the congregation about the discussions taking place and possible plans for some type of AIDS ministry. It was not common for the governing council to approve the programs of individual committees, though the council chair did advise the committee to provide adequate communication and education for the congregation.

The committee, now prepared to begin an AIDS Ministry, planned three Sundays when they would have a display at the coffee hour attended by most of the members, staffed by members of the committee. Their plans for this new ministry and the availability of their informational display booth were to be announced in the church bulletin and newsletter, along with the names and telephone numbers of all committee members. On the kickoff Sunday for this informational phase, the pastor, already hearing some rumblings of concern from the congregation, asked the committee chair to take time during the worship service announcements to say something about the committee's plans.

Here is what the committee chair said that morning:

"The social concerns committee plans to begin a new ministry at the heart of our mandate to engage the gospel with the needs of others. We see the need in our community for an AIDS Ministry serving those with AIDS, their loved ones, and the larger community through education regarding this devastating disease. To be quite honest, when the subject first came up in our committee, I had my reservations, not about the need, but about whether it was appropriate for our church to take the lead on this matter, given how emotionally charged it is for some persons.

"Then I remembered a story I first heard during new member orientation years ago when I transferred to this church. I am sure some of you know the story much better than I; perhaps some of you were involved or had family members involved. As I remember it, during the Great Depression, our church was the only church in the county to permit its buildings to be used for government programs on behalf of those in need throughout the region. In recalling that story, I realized, 'That's us.' At first, I was concerned that I did not know of any other church in our area with an AIDS Ministry. Now that fact does not bother me. In fact, that's who we are. We are people willing to be the first to do what others are reluctant to do—so long as it clearly is going to help other people in the name of Christ. Stepping out first for others is just who we are as a church."

Chapter 4

Identify Key Phases of Your Visioning Process

.

While it is true that when two or three are gathered together, Christ is present; it is also true that when two or three gather, you have an organization. Indeed, the very organizational nature of the church holds it together for ministry. Thus, the characteristics of organizational life and vitality have to be taken into account by the church, even as a church must take account of the characteristics of their church building as a physical facility. Just because it is a church, a community of believers is not exempt from the "laws" of organizations or buildings.

All organizations go through similar and predictable cycles over time. For one organization, the cycle may be complete within a short time. For another, the cycle might need to be viewed over centuries. Although the purpose of this book is to enable creative interventions in the cycle for renewal, the basic tendencies of organizational life as organizations mature must first be understood. The following outline of the general movement of organizations is one way to describe common phases of organizational life.

PHASES OF THRIVING AND DECLINING ORGANIZATIONS

Phase One: Original Vision

Here the vision is tightly focused. There is a fit between vision and need. It is a time of intense passion around the vision. The vision gets the most attention, energy, and time. When people come together in this period, all they talk about is the dream, because that is all they have. There is no structure; there is no building; there is nothing but the dream. The vision is as pure as it will ever be again. In this phase the only structures that are put together are those forms required for the vision to get a start, to become a reality.

Phase Two: Growth and Building the Organization

In this phase the organization does well in advancing the vision. It establishes a strong and growing position within its environment and in relationship to other similar organizations. The organization becomes more complex during this period. Those additional forms, structures, and buildings that are required—not only for the vision to become a reality but also for it to continue, grow, and make an impact—are put in place. Now when leaders come together, they still talk about the dream, but they have to give time to their structure, staffing, buildings, and other issues of organizational life.

Phase Three: Maintenance

As this phase begins, the organization continues to be successful and grow. However, more and more time and attention now must be given to maintaining an organization that is not only growing but also becoming more complex. The distance from the original vision, both historically and emotionally, grows greater. By the end of this period when peo-

76

ple come together, they find themselves saying, "It seems as if when we meet we talk about nothing but maintaining the organization. We never talk anymore about the original dream that brought us into being in the first place." And it is when concern for maintenance becomes inordinate that it leads to the next phase, which is decline.

Phase Four: Decline

At first the decline is only in the *rate of growth,* so *growth* is still continuing. However, the rate of growth in relation to the relevant environmental standards, such as population growth or economic growth, does not keep pace. Therefore, apparent growth is actually real decline. Then actual decline in numbers begins, well after the decline in *rate* of growth has begun.

Phase Five: Recognized Decline

This phase tends to come long after real decline has set in. Decline has continued long enough now that the illusion of a temporary setback, because of social, cultural, demographic, or economic changes, has been dispelled. Dramatic efforts to reverse the decline do not change the basic pattern. All the quick-fix rescue programs have been tried and have failed. Isolated examples of growth that have been seen as signs of renewal are now seen to be what they actually are, the exception that proves the rule. That which finally gets the attention and recognition of a problem by everyone comes from the worsening economic situation of the organization. It is only at this point that the reality of decline sets in for many people.

Phase Six: Crisis or Death

Normally, basic change only occurs out of organizational crisis. The worsening situation, after all attempts to explain,

77

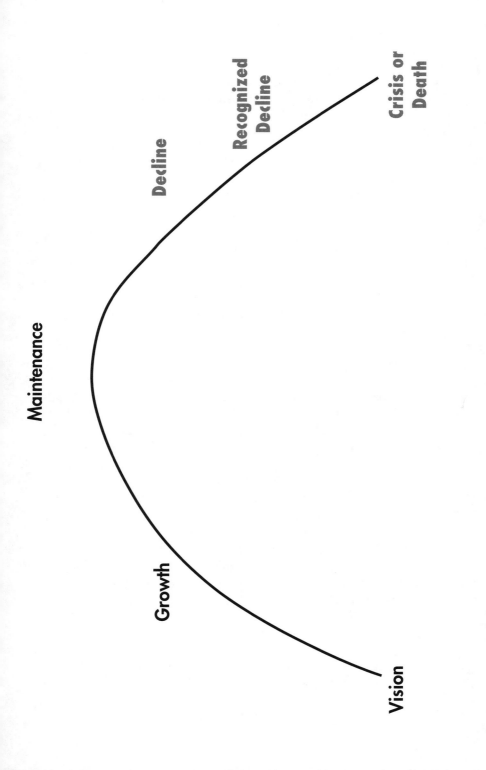

rationalize, and delay have been exhausted, leads to openness for a rethinking of how things are done. Otherwise, the alternative is death or, more likely, a prolonged existence that bears virtually no resemblance to the original vital organization.[1]

RENEWAL THROUGH REVISIONING IS POSSIBLE

The processes involved in the strengthening and weakening of human organizations are universal. However, the very nature of living systems is that renewal is possible. This can come through revisioning. Somewhere along the cycle, there comes a time when a new vision emerges. The new vision is consistent with the original vision, but it is also different. The new vision shares most with the original vision the power to inspire and motivate the membership. Therefore, a new upward cycle begins out of the power of the new vision. Indeed, it has all the feel of a "refounding." The time will come when that vision will also need to be renewed but for the immediate future, this will be the guiding star for a revitalized congregation.

SEARCHING FOR GOD'S VISION

Selecting and articulating the right vision, this powerful idea, is the toughest task and the truest test of great leadership.

Burt Nanus[2]

What is the secret behind discerning a captivating and fitting vision? There are no easy answers, but some patterns emerge from study. Denise Shekerjian, in an excellent study of forty winners of the Macarthur Award, concluded that the great ideas of the artists, scientists, and social activists were

79

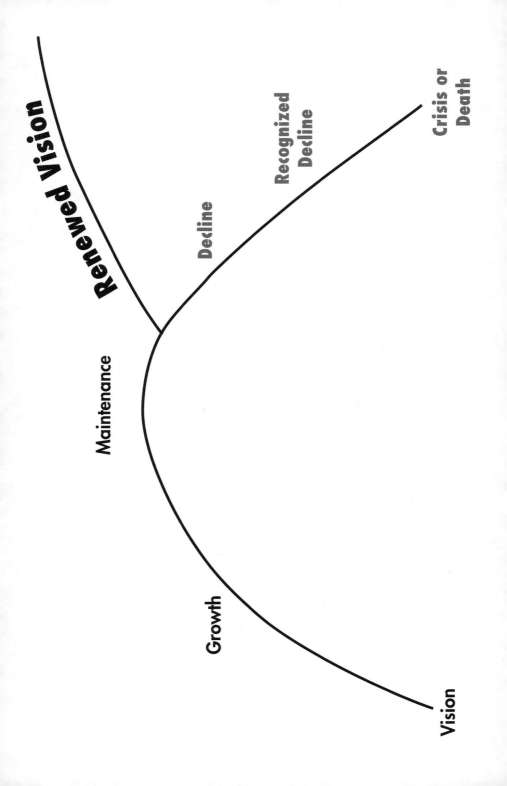

born of a combination of instinct and judgment. She says, "What intuition provides is an inkling, an itch, a yearning, a mist of possibilities. What judgment provides is structure, assessment, form, purpose."[3] As persons who honor the spiritual dimensions of life, we understand that true wisdom requires an outpouring of God's spirit; and we also know how structured disciplines and practices make it more likely that God's wisdom can be recognized.

Visioning is not a neat, orderly, and linear process any more than our Christian pilgrimage is. Some of what happens in visioning, even as in our life of discipleship, is even hard for us to explain after the fact. Those who do best at visioning tend to have at least some tolerance for ambiguity and uncertainty.

Vision is the common thread that leads us into the future. It is not a way to control a group. Just the opposite. It gives everyone an opportunity to participate in a common essential endeavor instead of wasting energy on a myriad of efforts that do not address the current needs out of the congregation's basic identity. The vision must connect with the deepest values, hopes, and dreams of the people and leaders. Only then will the vision be both right and capable of implementation.

Vision is a mental journey from the known to the unknown, creating the future from the montage of current facts, hopes, dreams, dangers, and opportunities that effective leaders embrace in all walks of life.
Craig R. Hickman and Michael A. Silva[4]

LISTENING WITH A SPIRITUAL EAR

Dorothy Smith, a seminary student preaching in chapel shortly before her graduation, used a phrase that caught my imagination. She talked about "listening with a spiritual ear." I realized that was the listening that effective church leaders do. It is the ability to listen at a level deeper than the surface and most obvious meanings.

Burt Nanus talks about this as listening "carefully for quiet whisperings in dark corners."[5] Margaret Wheatley refers to this gift as "harvesting the invisible intelligence" that exists within the organization.[6] Heifetz and Linsky talk about listening to the "song beneath the words."

There are many reasons why listening must take place at a deeper level than a mere compilation of comments. Most people cannot frame fully formed visions, but they can give the clues out of which visions emerge. Most people have limited experience and knowledge. A person may be a patient in a hospital for a long period of time and, therefore, is in a good position to give feedback about the hospital. But, in reality, that patient has had a markedly limited experience of the hospital as a whole. The patient can give exceedingly helpful advice about a part of the hospital's work, but is not in a position to give a complete evaluation of the overall mission and performance of the hospital.

So it is with churches. Most will know certain dimensions of congregational life extremely well, with other parts remaining much less familiar if known at all. In a similar vein, people are able to give input out of their own life situation but may not be helpful in putting that information in the larger context of a more diverse congregation. If listening were only a tallying of concerns and issues, then that would lead merely to a list of problems to be solved. As we will see when we examine negative clues, those suggestions need to be heeded; but there must be a deeper listening going on in the visioning process.

Hearing what is not being said is one of the great arts of listening. This includes what is being omitted as well as what lies beneath the words being said. For example, Susan Sonnenday Vogel suggests a practice to use when people are offering negative opinions or resisting some direction. As a way of hearing what is beneath the words, one can ask, "What is it to which they are saying 'yes' in their comments?" Instead of focusing on what they are against, one can ask what is the competing value or commitment that causes them to talk in these negative terms.

James Madison encouraged leaders to listen to the stated aspirations of people but then seek to "discern the true interests" and to ascertain the underlying needs they have in common with others but are unable to articulate on their own. Leaders then can "refine and enlarge the public views" and rephrase them in a way that transcends the contradictions among the people and the more self-serving narrow interests present. Madison believed it was possible that this reframed "public voice" would be "more consonant to the public good than if pronounced by the people themselves." James O'Toole extends Madison's thoughts to say that once leaders have discovered the underlying needs of followers, they then can help "create a new, transcendent vision that not only is large enough to encompass the variety of needs but, more important, elevates petty personal desires to the nobler level of a common good."[7]

VISION IS NOT CREATED BUT DISCOVERED

Vision is not created. It is discovered or, more precisely for people of faith, discerned. Major sources for this discovery and discernment process are the clues that are all around us every day. Winston Churchill once said that some people stumble over the truth and then get up, dust themselves off, and go on their way. That is how some people fail to notice profound clues for visioning that God provides near us all the time.

Visioning is not a gift of greater wisdom or intelligence but rather of observation, probing, synthesis, intuition, and creativity; in other words, visioning is a process of spiritual discernment.

The clues for vision are discovered in the midst of daily activities, not necessarily apart from those responsibilities. Clues for visioning are found on the way to daily faithfulness. Clues for the big picture God has for us are discovered in the specifics of life that may seem on the surface utterly insignificant.

These clues are available to many people, but only some actually see them. The genius of visionary leadership is in recognizing those clues, putting them together with other clues, and then testing those clues with others to make sure that one is seeing and hearing correctly or that one is putting the different clues together in a manner that makes sense.

During the summer of 1943, Edwin and Helen Land were vacationing in New Mexico with their three-year-old daughter, Jennifer. Edwin Land was an executive and researcher with the Polaroid Corporation. One day he took a picture of Jennifer. After the shutter clicked, Jennifer wanted to see her picture. She could not understand why she could not see the snapshot immediately.

Land's first instinct was to explain the "reality" of the situation to his daughter. Surely he could help her understand that it was utterly impossible to see a picture immediately after it is taken. Fortunately, the three-year-old's uninformed question became just the opportunity for Land to say "Why not?"

Land later recalled that within an hour after Jennifer's question, the camera, film, and physical chemistry required for "instant images" became clear enough "that with a great sense of excitement I hurried to the place where a friend was staying, to describe to him in detail a dry camera which would give a picture immediately after exposure."

So was the birth of instant photography. One might say, "Luck." However, in reality, everything in Land's life had been preparing him to hear his daughter's question in a special way. His education, business and technical background, and research qualifications helped him take what could have

84

been seen as yet another silly question by a young child and see in it the making of a great vision. Still, Land had to *recognize* the clue. Would all similarly prepared workers in the photography industry have responded in the same manner? Clearly not. "All that we at Polaroid had learned," he later said, "was like preparation for that day in which I suddenly knew how to make a one-step photographic process." The simple question by his daughter caused him to bring together many things that he knew but had not put together in quite the same way until he heard that question and, from it, developed the first Polaroid Land Camera.[8]

What might this look like for a church leader? There is a meeting at which many people are present and virtually everyone contributes to the discussion of a particular issue. During the meeting a youth makes a particular comment. Everyone listens and then others continue speaking. The following day few, if any, of the people from the meeting can remember what this youth said except for one member of the group. This leader could not keep from thinking about the comment because of a statement that had been heard two nights before at another unrelated meeting. This comment also connected with something that emerged out of a national church survey that had been read a few weeks earlier. The comment connected as well with a passage of scripture read in a morning devotional recently and, perhaps most significantly for this person, it connected with something the person's adult child, who had been out of church since leaving home, had said during a recent visit home.

LOOKING FOR CLUES

"Clue management" is what Michael Kami calls "the practice of reading between the lines and detecting trends."[9] Leaders are always looking for clues.

It is not information of a general sort that helps a President . . . not summaries, not surveys, not the bland amalgams. Rather it is the odds and ends of tangible detail that pieced together in his mind illuminate the underside of issues put before him. To help himself, he must reach out as widely as he can for every scrap of fact, opinion, gossip, bearing on his interests and relationships as President. He must become his own director of his own central intelligence.

Richard E. Neustadt[10]

Becky Haase tells a story out of her experience that illustrates the power of noticing clues.

In 1994, Becky's home was within the area affected by the Northridge, California, earthquake. Their electricity was off for six hours. A neighbor noticed that when the lights in all the homes went out, there was still a light in one room of the Haase home. The source was a light that goes on when the power goes off. The neighbor said, "I want to get one of those!" Becky then decided to buy two additional ones as gifts for upcoming family birthdays.

Becky waited a week because crowds in stores were heavy following the earthquake. When she went to the store and asked if they still had the same light, the clerk said, "I think so, but I am not sure where they are."

Finally, with another clerk's help, they were able to find some of the lights in a section with such things as industrial batteries. There appeared to be about twenty-five in stock, so Becky bought several—for all members of her family. The clerk who was helping her bought one for herself at the same time. At the checkout stand the clerk suggested to the cashier that she buy one also.

A few days later Becky saw in the newspaper the store's advertisement for these lights. When another friend went to purchase a light, she discovered that they had sold out. They assured her they had ordered more—one thousand more! Good leaders are always alert to clues—clues that reveal unexpected interest, unanticipated energy, or surprising responses.

NEGATIVE CLUES AND POSITIVE CLUES

Negative Clues

Both negative clues and positive clues are always present. Both are extremely important, but they are different and require quite different responses.

Examples of negative clues include such things as concern about spending policies, length of the worship service, size of the staff, and difficulty finding a place to park. They represent some of the concerns and challenges that are always present.

Leaders must be responsive (though not reactive) to negative clues, even if what is being said is not technically correct. This does not mean that one does exactly what people are asking, but there definitely must be a responsive spirit showing that the concerns are being taken seriously. If there is not such a responsive attitude, and the concern is ignored or devalued, then these feelings and the people who hold them will come back to haunt leaders later. Therefore, it is crucial to be responsive to negative clues, but it is also imperative to remember that one cannot build a great future just on negative clues. Even as one is being responsive to negative clues, there must be passionate pursuit of positive clues.

For example, let's assume the negative clue comes as persistent grumbling because the worship service is going well beyond what the membership feels is the common understanding about the ending time for the service. Some way must be found to be responsive to this concern. It may be in shortening the service or renegotiating the shared assumptions, but attention must be given or it can lead to later sabotage. As this negative clue is being addressed, a leader does not forget that even if the church established a direct link with the Naval Observatory to assure accurate timekeeping and set a foolproof plan that assured that the worship service would never go overtime, that alone would not guarantee that God's reign would prevail in that community!

How tempting it is to put all of our efforts into dealing with a series of negative clues that come at us constantly and, in doing so, never have time or energy left to respond to the positive clues or perhaps even to notice them. And the saddest thing is that we can actually convince ourselves that we are doing something. Actually, we are doing something, but in the priorities of our mission, not much. Responding to negative clues is absolutely essential but, alone, absolutely inadequate.

Positive Clues

It is essential to find some positive clue, value, or direction on which to build the future. Another way to think about negative and positive clues is to think of them as the "dying edges" and "living edges" of the church. What are those things which seem to have lost their life, are hard to promote, or do not generate energy? Similarly, what are those things that even without promotion always do well? Where is there life and energy within the congregation? What are the types of things about which people are excited? What are the things that have to be promoted inordinately and still barely go?

Locating living edges is always a key task for a leader. Where is there life, energy, and power? Only then can one discover clues from those living edges. What characteristics do they have in common? Why are people finding meaning and offering commitment in these ways?

A useful exercise for a leader is to make a list of some of the dying edges and living edges in the congregation. Then, one can look at each of the two lists and come up with the characteristics the items in each separate list have in common with each other, and compare the characteristics of the two lists. This should give a clue about what is likely to do well or not do well with future efforts. If the new endeavor shares the basic characteristics of the living edges, it is likely to succeed. If the new effort shares the characteristics of the dying edges, success is not likely.

Positive clues may not always appear positive at first. They actually may be negative in content but positive in terms of needs and opportunities for mission. Discovering that a county has the highest rate of adult illiteracy in the state is a negative statistic, but it may be just the clue to point toward an appropriate mission direction for a congregation.

CHAOS AND VISIONING

"Creation comes out of chaos," says Parker Palmer, and "even what has been created needs to be returned to chaos every now and then to get recreated in a more vital form."[11] On Renaissance maps the words "Here be dragons!" were inscribed "to mark the limits of the then-known world and to warn explorers foolhardy enough to want to venture beyond them."[12] Although those words make us smile, we also know that the unknown is not our favorite arena. We understand, with Parker Palmer, that creation comes out of chaos; but the comfort we feel with the order of creation as we know it makes the prospect of returning to chaos for a renewed creation scary.

Yet as Margaret Wheatley has told us, "In order to thrive in a world of change and chaos, we will need to accept chaos as an essential process by which natural systems, including organizations, renew and revitalize themselves."[13] Maybe Mitchell Waldrop's term "edge of chaos" is more descriptive.

Change does not come out of utter chaos but rather from living where there is enough stability to sustain the organization but also far enough from the stagnation of rigid order for the creativity and experimentation that can lead to change.[14]

Without some disequilibria in the system, there would be death, even as a straight line on a heart monitor is not a good sign. Not withstanding this reality, our natural tendency is to overreact to chaos in the system instead of understanding it for what it is, a valuable source of clues for the present and the future. Understanding is needed more than judgment. The most wonderful discovery of embracing chaos is that not only can we survive but also we can thrive by opening ourselves and our congregation to new possibilities.

Chapter 5

A Model for Visioning

Visioning is not a simple undertaking. In retrospect, it may seem simple because the results appear clear and obvious. Yet, the process that leads to the simple vision is often complex, intuitive, circuitous, and foundationally spiritual. The route to a vision is rarely direct, obvious, or uniform. It is helpful to remember that visioning is, at its essence, a process of discernment.

Therefore, any model for visioning will, of necessity, tend to oversimplify and make a complex process appear much more orderly than can ever be the case. All one can do is to extract from a model the fundamental nature of it, apply it in what appears to be a fitting way for each situation, and realize that reality does not always replicate models as one might wish. The spirit, direction, and essential elements of any model will need to be understood; then they can be adjusted without losing the critical dimensions that made this model helpful for others.

As with any discernment process, while one cannot orchestrate guaranteed success, there are some relatively basic and simple steps that one can go through that make success far more likely. Writers and preachers learn this lesson quite early. This model is an attempt to provide a resource to help congregations get started in visioning. The effort here is not to reduce visioning to a formula or set of steps that assure success. Such is never possible. Rather, the following suggestions are intended to set the stage for people to talk together about the questions from which visions often emerge.

DIFFERENCE BETWEEN MISSION AND VISION

Mission and vision, as used here, are related but not synonymous.[1] Mission is what God calls the church to do. It is the purpose of a church. It is its reason for being.

Vision, on the other hand, while grounded in the mission, is that to which God is calling the congregation to do in the near future to advance the mission. What is the most compelling need facing the congregation if it is to be faithful to what God has called this church to do? Discovering God's vision for one's church comes by asking, "Given the mission of our congregation and the current situation, what is it that God is most calling this church to do next?" Vision is the content of the congregation's next chapter.

A particular church's mission statement may read, "To share and model Christ to our community and the world." However, because of an unfortunate set of circumstances surrounding the departure of the last pastor six months earlier, the congregation is badly divided. At least half the members have quit attending. Those who continue are almost equally divided over the action of the church that led to the pastor's leaving. The situation is badly polarized, and few attempts have been made to resolve the difficulties. An elaborate visioning process is not needed to see that the vision for this congregation is healing and reconciliation. A year before, this would not have emerged as the vision. Moreover, if this vision of healing is successful, three years later this vision will no longer be appropriate. Yet, right now the division of the congregation makes the fulfillment of the stated mission utterly impossible without engaging the vision of healing. In fact, the negative witness of the congregation, without success with this new vision, may actually be doing harm to the cause of Christ in their community.

Mission or Vision?

(A laywoman reports how clarifying the difference between mission and vision helped her ministry team move forward effectively.)

I have been chairing the community program that feeds children during the summer at no cost. These are the children who receive free and reduced-cost lunches during the school year. We had just completed year five, and we had experienced a LOT of changes this year (new location, "competition" from summer school, new staff, different volunteers). We were trying to evaluate whether the program should (a) continue as is, or (b) change, and if so, how?

One person talked about how the core of people who had the original vision for this project (except for a few of us) were no longer involved and questioned whether we had "lost the vision" of the effort. One thing led to another, and then I said "a mission is what we exist to do (feed children), and the vision is what God is most calling us to do at this point in time in light of the mission."

I went on to explain that the vision of bringing children to the church may no longer be the best way to feed children in the summer. The best way may be to see to it that they get to summer school (provide transportation) so they can receive the free/reduced-cost lunch there and receive enrichment and remedial courses as well.

Everyone thought that the mission/vision explanation was just wonderful and asked me to repeat it so they could all write it down!

We ended the meeting by deciding that pursuing

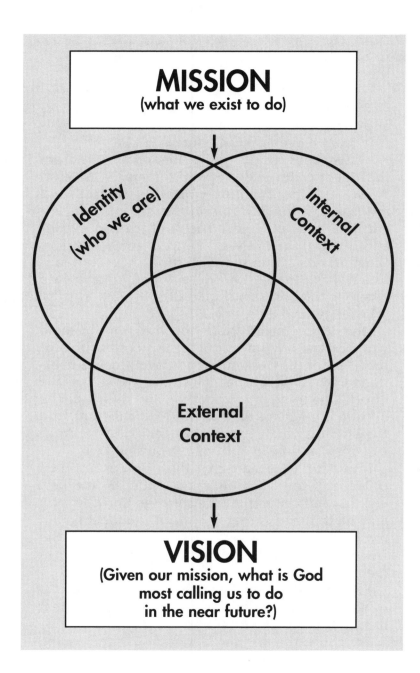

more church support was perhaps not the only way to go and that partnering with the schools might be worth pursuing.

MISSION—WHAT A CHURCH EXISTS TO DO

A mission statement should be one simple sentence that states clearly and succinctly what an organization exists to do. The mission represents an organization's reason for being.

While mission is essential, it is not adequate by itself. Often a mission for one church is similar to the mission of another congregation. That should not be a surprise. However, the circumstances between those two churches require something more than a mission statement. There must also be a vision for what that mission statement means just now for each individual congregation. Together mission and vision make a powerful combination. Efforts are rooted in the very essence of the purpose of the church, yet they are also addressing what is most needed for faithful witness here and now.

A congregation needs to address a number of elements in order to get to the compelling vision for just now. This model seeks input for visioning in three crucial categories: congregational identity, internal congregational context, and external congregational context.

CONGREGATIONAL IDENTITY (WHO YOU ARE)

Identity represents who you are, what you have been, what you believe, and what you value. It includes the congregation's mission but includes much more.

Core Values

Values describe the commitments of any organization that shape the way the organization does its work. If the mission defines what the organization will do, values describe the commitments that will be honored in the fulfillment of the mission. In some ways the values represent the guidelines and boundaries within which the organization will function to accomplish the mission. These commitments will shape how the congregation carries out its mission. Sorting out core values will help everyone get clear about what is truly important to this congregation. Each congregation has its distinct sacred bundle of core values. Some may not be lived out consistently, but those values still have great power if they are a part of how the congregation most sees itself. Values, like mission, will tend to stay fixed over a long period, although visions will need to change to meet new circumstances.

Richard Southern and Robert Norton suggest a three-step process for identifying congregational core values out of the many worthy values that might be suggested by church members:

> *Identify* those three to five values that are an essential part of the life and work of your congregation.
> *Define*—in writing—exactly what each of these values means in the life of your congregation.
> *Prioritize* them, because they have varying degrees of importance and meaning in the life of your congregation.[2]

History

Look to the rock from which you were hewn, and to the quarry from which you were dug.

Isaiah 51:1*b*

Vision will always grow out of the history of the congregation. It is important to understand the flow of history that brought the congregation to its current state. It helps to reflect on some key historical events in the life of the church and to understand how they have shaped and affected the congregation.

A helpful way for a group to appropriate their history in order to inform and shape visioning is to do a history timeline. There are many ways to do this. One way is simply to draw a long horizontal line with the year the church began on one end and the current year on the other. Then the leader can ask people in the group to put a mark on the timeline to show when they entered the life of the church and describe what was happening at that time. During the discussion, others who entered the church around that time may participate. Then others in the group who entered before or after will describe another period of time. As they write important words from their descriptions on the timeline, they can also write above and below the timeline other important information to match the historical periods they are describing. Such information might include who the pastors were. Another strand running across might be important events happening in the community, nation, and world during different eras.

Participants may even describe the time before the birth of present members because there will be people there who will know of the history through parents and grandparents, or by studying the history of the church. As a group works on the timeline, distinct chapters in the church's history will emerge. In addition, everyone will begin to understand in a deeper way how the church came to be the way it is today and what the positive and negative implications are for moving into the future.

Cultural Heritage

Each congregation has its own unique cultural heritage, which was described in chapter 3. The congregational culture brings together denominational, liturgical, regional, ethnic, class, and other traditions and characteristics that shape the character of this church.

INTERNAL CONGREGATIONAL CONTEXT (WHAT'S GOING ON WITHIN THE CHURCH?)

Needs: Short-Range, Mid-Range, Long-Range

What are the concerns and issues present within the church that most require attention? It is important not merely to focus on the most immediate needs but to think of various periods of time. Some questions to get at these issues are:

Short-Range Issues—What needs/issues should be addressed in the next twelve months?

Mid-Range Issues—What are the most important issues/needs that will affect our church significantly five years from now?

Long-Range Issues—What are the most important issues/needs that will affect our church significantly ten years from now?

The specific time frame for each question may need to be different from church to church. Perhaps it is clear that a more concise time frame (such as one year, three years, five years) may be needed, but it is important to have people thinking beyond only the current pressing matters.

Key Strengths

It is also important to clarify those distinctive gifts of a congregation that give clues about what the church is reasonably capable of accomplishing. For what are we rightfully known? What do we really have going for us? Experience indicates that using different questions to come at key strengths from slightly different angles will elicit a more complete picture of the major assets of the church.

98

Some questions to use are:

Hope Never Changes: "What is so good about our church that you hope it never changes?"

Do Well: "What does our church do as well as any church anywhere?"

Strengths: "What are the three greatest strengths of our church?"

Doing a SWOT Analysis

Some find it helpful to use in their visioning a SWOT analysis—the assessment of congregational Strengths, Weaknesses, Opportunities, and Threats. If this type of analysis is done of the congregation, it should also be done of the external context in which the church functions so the results can be compared. To do one without the other may result in some misleading conclusions.

Statistics and Trends

For visioning to be effective, dependable data are needed in an accessible format. For the congregation's internal context, some of the data to collect may include statistics related to such things as worship, church school, budget, finances, demographics, space, staffing, and participation levels for various ministries.

A useful way to collect the various tables and statistics is a trends data book. It is usually best to seek information for the past five to ten years. This makes it possible to see changes and trends. The goal is to look for clues, hints, hunches, and insights about the future and about planning for that future. Many people need to be involved in this process. Different eyes will spot different things. It will be critically important to look for what discoveries tend to be made repeatedly by different people and groups looking at the same material.

Preparing a trends data book for the external context is

also useful. Preparing one comprehensive trends data book containing information about both the internal congregational data as well as the external data about the community permits people to work in many small groups to identify trends and clues for the future. It is essential that that people are working with the same trusted information. Without such data, plans may be made on the basis of faulty assumptions about the past. The past is often remembered quite differently from what the statistics show to have been the situation. Trusted data helps define a true and shared baseline from which decisions can be made.

Opinions and Perceptions

As important as statistics are, those opinions, perceptions, and ideas people have about the congregation are equally important. Such feedback regarding the current situation and future needs of the church's ministries is essential in visioning. Conversations, surveys, and small group discussions are some means often used to get at this source for visioning.

There is the need to get good feedback regarding specific areas (e.g., worship, education), and particular components of each (e.g., which components of the worship service mean most to parishioners, how do people evaluate different educational opportunities). There is also a need for open-ended questions, such as: If you could wave a magic wand and change one thing about our church, what would you change? What about our church is most important to you? What do you find least important about our church?

Clues in Small Things

Much can be learned from simply paying attention. Tom Frank talks about paying attention as a spiritual discipline.[3] Simply being present and involved with the people of the church will turn up important clues for the careful observer and listener.

EXTERNAL CONGREGATIONAL CONTEXT
(WHAT'S GOING ON AROUND YOU?)

Responsiveness to the environment and to the changes taking place around an organization is probably the most fundamental requirement of leadership.

Harry Levinson[4]

What is going on in the external environment in which the church functions? What is anticipated in the future? Effective leaders of change are adept at identifying clues for the future and anticipating changes that are on the horizon. This is one way to sense problems before they have become unmanageable. Often churches have difficulty taking into account changes that have been present for several years, much less anticipating those changes that may be coming. This is why becoming attuned to environment is crucial. The task of identifying changes and trends is key both within the congregational review and the external context analysis.

Statistics and Trends

Collecting data on the congregation's external context is similar to the approach used for internal congregational data. Some information to seek may include such things as population figures, demographic breakdowns, economic statistics, denominational and judicatory membership, as well as attendance statistics, traffic patterns, and trends occurring in other comparable churches.

As with internal data, it is good to collect information for the past five to ten years in order to identify changes and trends. The result of working with the data is to identify insights to be used in planning for the future. Broad participation in reviewing the data for clues is needed since differ-

101

ent eyes will notice different things. Perhaps the most important reason for involving many people is to spot the discoveries made repeatedly by different people and groups looking at the same material.

Including data for the congregation's external context in the trends data book is critical. This permits people to compare congregational trends with community trends. For example, there may be a concern about youth participation in church. The trends data book may indicate that youth participation as a percentage of community population has not changed in the past ten years, but that another age group is significantly underrepresented in the congregation based on the data studied.

Who's Missing?

A team was formed from the visioning task force to work with demographics. They studied population statistics and enrollment patterns in their school district. They obtained census information for the zip code in which the church was located. As they looked at figures over the last twenty years, they saw some clear demographic shifts.

Whites were leaving the area and African Americans were moving into the area. The whites that remained tended to be older persons. The school enrollment was growing at the same time the local church membership and attendance had been declining, particularly among school age children. The zip code analysis showed that the age breakdown of the population tilted to the younger side as the congregation was aging. Their zip code had a higher percentage of every age group until the age of fifty, after which the area had a lower percentage, when compared to state and US averages. They were especially struck by the high percentage in their zip code of the youngest age category, birth to five years.

The clue that eventually emerged from this visioning process was around African American children. For twenty years the congregation had had African American members and leaders, but they still did not have African American children participating. They concluded that if this congregation was to have a vital future in that community, then its future lay in finding ways to connect their message with African American children and their families.

Doing a SWOT Analysis

An analysis of environmental Strengths, Weaknesses, Opportunities, and Threats is a needed complement to the similar analysis of the congregation. It is the environmental assessment that will tend often to get less consideration, if any at all, when planning decisions are made. Churches invariably tend to underestimate the influence of contextual issues upon them as if they alone will be the one institution that is not affected by clear trends or issues in the larger surrounding environment.

Choosing the One Most Important Focus

During a visioning process a congregation had done an excellent job of identifying the most pressing issues facing the church in the coming years. Careful survey work, focus groups, and visioning team analysis found six areas needing major attention. Some of them were declining membership, declining financial resources, loss of population, declining payment of their denominational mission support, deferred maintenance, and reaching younger people.

The process had been a bit dispiriting for them as they realized how many negatives they had working against them as they sought to reverse a long trend of decline in a once strong congregation. They now had to decide around which need the vision would center. Focusing on six things at once would be business as usual. They broke into groups for discussion; but when the groups reported, there was no consensus. Their discussions had simply reflected different perspectives on which of the items were most important to different groups.

Then, a visiting consultant who had been working with them suggested they go back into their groups with a different assignment. "If you had to leave this meeting and go meet with four different members or families who are not on the visioning team to announce to them the focus of our new vision," the consultant asked them, "which of these issues, if it were that focus, would give them most hope for the future of their congregation?" With this new assignment, they returned to their groups. When they reported, every single group came back with "reaching younger people" as the focus for the vision. All the other issues will need to be addressed, but they can be addressed "on the way" to fulfilling this vision.

Opinions and Perceptions

Much less attention is normally given to external perceptions of the congregation than internal perceptions. Both are important. It is key to get a sense of how the community perceives the church and its ministry. Some churches have gained this information by inviting persons from the community who are not members of their own church to give an hour or two in helping the church identify the needs of the community as well as getting a reading about how the church is perceived within the community. This group can normally be gathered by asking some church members to invite their friends.

Other churches gather this information by assigning some members to ask a few questions of different community constituents. Some questions to use include: When you think of Trinity Church, what first comes to mind? With what ministries do you associate Trinity Church? If someone asked you to describe Trinity Church, what would you say?

Clues in Small Things

Just as with the internal context, much can be learned from simply paying attention to clues about the external environment.

Where's the Church?

A visitor came to town for a meeting at one of the local churches. Knowing that the town was relatively small and that the church was located generally within the main business area of the town, the visitor did not request specific directions to the church ahead of time. Upon arriving in the town and driving around, the visitor discovered the church location was not obvious. The visitor stopped at a convenience store to ask directions to the church. No one there knew where it was. The visitor asked a passerby on the street. No luck. The visitor went into a café to inquire about directions. Still, no one knew the location of the church. The visitor then went to the post office and found someone who did know the location. It turned out that the church was within two blocks of all the people who were asked the location and did not know where the church was.

If this visitor, upon arrival at the meeting, shares this experience with the host from this congregation, there is an opportunity either to ignore this clue or to find in this series of events a gigantic message to this church that, despite being in this community for more than 100 years, it has become virtually invisible to the residents.

GATHERING INPUT FOR THE VISIONING PROCESS

What is the best way to get the information needed for this visioning process? There are many ways. In fact, a diversity of means of collecting these insights from a congregation will make the process more interesting and beneficial. For example, small group discussion might work well for one part. Another component might be done with a simple half-sheet, three-question survey included in the Sunday worship bulletin with a brief time set aside in the service for completion in order to maximize response. A session with the governing board of the church or all church officers could work for yet another part. The process that will produce the best and most representative and reliable information should be chosen.

INTERLOCKING CIRCLES

Many people find the use of interlocking circles to be a useful device to help themselves and groups see clues, and especially recurring themes, that emerge from different but related topics and questions. Interlocking circles permit people to locate common themes that normally indicate a direction that should be pursued, heeded, or honored. The purpose of interlocking circles is not so much to exclude what is not held in common among the circles but to identify the common issues that must come first. Other things may very well be done, but one does not build the life of the church around those less central issues. There are many minor things that need to be done, should be done, and will be done. However, in doing all those things, the sum will not likely be a renewed church.

For example, in a given day a person may have several

106

errands and tasks that need to be done—stopping by the cleaners, picking up a few items at the grocery store, and mailing a bill payment. All these things need to be done and will be done. However, those tasks do not constitute the essence of the person's day. These errands are not permitted to define life for that day. The person finds a way for the smaller yet necessary tasks to take an appropriate place within a larger picture. So it is with a host of things that must be done within the church; but through visioning and planning, these tasks are put in perspective.

STRENGTH IN RECURRING THEMES

For each set of interlocking circles, the goal is to identify the common themes, words, phrases, concepts, issues, and images. A vision emerging from these will be much more likely to be rooted in the heart of identity and the internal and external contexts.

The illustration on the next page shows how one congregation used interlocking circles to identify the recurring themes related to their most pressing congregational needs for the future.

VISION

I am about to do a new thing; now it springs forth, do you not perceive it?

Isaiah 43:19*a*

The concept of "vision" may seem overused, but nothing is more critical to successful leadership than the discernment and implementation of the appropriate vision for the "appointed time," to use the language from Habakkuk. Vision emerges from the intersection of congregational identity (mission, values, heritage), internal congregational context (needs, strengths, trends), and the external

IDENTIFIED CONGREGATIONAL NEEDS

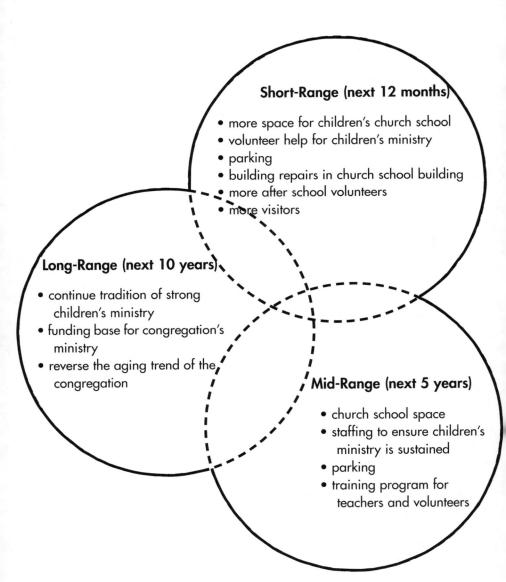

Short-Range (next 12 months)
- more space for children's church school
- volunteer help for children's ministry
- parking
- building repairs in church school building
- more after school volunteers
- more visitors

Long-Range (next 10 years)
- continue tradition of strong children's ministry
- funding base for congregation's ministry
- reverse the aging trend of the congregation

Mid-Range (next 5 years)
- church school space
- staffing to ensure children's ministry is sustained
- parking
- training program for teachers and volunteers

congregational context (needs, opportunities, trends). The linking of these components helps to ensure both continuity and change. God's new future for churches is always connected to the past. Indeed, identifying the areas of continuity that can serve as the bridge to the next chapter in a church's history is an essential task.

WHO NAMES THE VISION?

Sometimes people will ask, "Does a vision come from a leader, or does it emerge from the grassroots?" The answer is that it does not matter as long as it is the right vision. Whether it is named by an individual or a more collective process, if it is not rooted in the identity of the congregation and does not make sense for what the congregation is facing at the moment, it will not ring true and will not stick. By the same token, if the vision does cause people to identify with it because the vision touches something they know to be right, they will not ask about the process anymore than people ask about the mechanics of sermon preparation when they are touched deeply by a sermon. "Does it ring true?" is always the question.

Vision is a gift of God given to the people of God. Often the pastor or another leader will first articulate a vision. This is true not so much because of position but because of access to many of the clues and conversations going on during the visioning process. Even in these cases, the vision almost never first appears fully formed. It is by going public with a possible vision that leaders often pick up the missing pieces of the puzzle that will lead eventually to the ultimate vision.

A Church Afire

Our council chairperson birthed the vision of "A Church Afire" during our visioning process. A visiting speaker challenged us to recall a time when First Church was most alive. The chairperson recalled a chapter from the church's history, 1895–1899. In December of 1895, the church was destroyed by fire. Twenty-four hours later the congregation came together to vote on whether to rebuild. Times were hard. Money was tight. Despite the obstacles, the church voted to rebuild. After the vote, a member of the congregation came forward to the chair's table. She removed her expensive jewelry and placed it on the table as the first contribution to the new church building. Others followed. In weeks, funds were in place by asking people to contribute the cost of each brick.

After two building phases, four years later the present sanctuary was opened. The church continued to pay all its denominational support during those four years. That story has become our vision to be captured today by the same spirit of daring and discipleship found in the church during that moment in our history, thus the vision theme: "A Church Afire." Plans to incorporate the vision include returning to the YMCA where the church met for the four years of building for a celebration event and asking a member to write a drama about the fire and the decision to rebuild.

WHO DOES THE VISIONING?

Who is involved in the visioning? The key is to get the wisdom of everyone, to make sure the interests of all are represented in the vision. The power is in the content of the vision not the exact process. Clearly, governance issues cannot be ignored, but the number of votes will not determine the power of the vision. To ignore governance mechanisms may serve to sabotage the vision even if it has great worth. But a unanimously approved vision that does not connect to the heart and soul of the congregation and the current situation will not lead to revitalization. A manageably sized group of accountable leaders and creative people can normally develop a truly inclusive plan to involve and guide a congregation through a visioning process.

One congregation thought they had discerned God's vision for them. They had spent much time and prayer seeking an appropriate vision for their next chapter. While there seemed to be consensus within the governing council of the church, some were reluctant to take a final vote. There may be something we have missed or some groups we have not consulted adequately, they maintained. A member of the group came up with a marvelous idea. "Why don't we consider this our 'tentative vision statement,' and post it on newsprint around the church so if we have missed something, we will find out. In the meantime, let's begin our new vision." One year later the hand-printed "tentative vision statement" was still up with everyone functioning well based on the vision. Leaders find ways to honor procedures and concerns people have but also keep moving forward where God seems to be leading the congregation.

Chapter 6

Take the Next Step

*If the goal is to write a new chapter in the congre-
gation's story, then it is essential that the story be
thoroughly understood and respected, and that the
new chapter pick up and advance the plot.*

David Clewell

Change is not becoming something entirely new. It is
becoming more of what we have been. It is also not
merely repeating the past; leadership helps people
draw from their heritage what is most needed for the current
day and then translate that heritage for a new time. For the
heritage to be useful for the future, it must be, as George
Thompson has put it, "released out of the past."[1] David
Clewell, in a doctor of ministry project, captures this concept well in the quotation that begins this chapter. His full
statement is: "If the goal is to write a new chapter in the congregation's story, then it is essential that the story be thoroughly understood and respected, and that the new chapter
pick up and *advance the plot*, language, themes and charac-
ters that have made up the previous chapters."

VIEW CHANGE FROM THE
PERSPECTIVE OF OTHERS

A key task for any church leader is the ability to see things
from the perspective of those in the congregation. It is by
seeing the change from the perspective of the congregation's
values and interests that a leader is able to frame the pro-

posed change in a way that is consistent with the church's culture. This also permits the leader to understand better what is at stake for others, including the nature of their fears, questions, and sense of loss. A leader tries always to see things from the perspectives of those on the receiving end of change.

Change leaders anticipate the questions of others before they are asked. They understand the concerns of various groups within the congregation. They name the concerns openly and identify with the concerns of others to the extent possible. This permits the leader to be responsive to the concerns rather than being reactive and abandoning the goals of the new vision.

What are the groups that have a stake in the change? If I put myself in their shoes, what would I think? What questions would I have? What would I have a right to expect regarding the change process?

A computer scientist from Stanford spent a year scanning with a laser light Michelangelo sculptures in Italy. But it took the naked eye and the use of scaffolding to detect some of the most revealing aspects of Michelangelo's *David*. Marc Levoy discovered that the two eyes of David are pointed in different directions. And the famous furrowed brow is anatomically impossible. How can one explain these seemingly unusual features? Michelangelo knew, according to Levoy, how far people would be away from the sculpture and from what direction light would be coming and, thus, designed the sculpture from the perspective of those who would view it. It was crafted based on how people would be seeing it![2]

Seven Unchangeable Rules of Change

People do what they perceive is in their best interest, thinking as rationally as circumstances allow them to think.

People are not inherently anti-change. Most will, in fact, embrace initiatives provided the change has positive meaning for them.

People thrive under creative challenge, but wilt under negative stress.

People are different. No single "elegant solution" will address the entire breadth of these differences.

People believe what they see. Actions do speak louder than words, and a history of previous deception octuples present suspicion.

The way to make effective long-term change is first to visualize what you want to accomplish, and then inhabit this vision until it comes true.

Change is an act of the imagination. Until the imagination is engaged, no important change can occur.

Harvey Robbins and Michael Finley[3]

PACING CHANGE AND REGULATING PAIN

You never know how hard change is until it is a change that was not your idea. For those of us in leadership, most of the changes we have to live with are our own ideas. All like change when it is their idea.

Brian McLaren[4]

Implementing change is not a smooth process. It can even be painful. Leaders must diligently watch the level of stress present in order to maintain a balance between too much and not enough. People can take change better in incremental steps, according to Donald L. Laurie. Too much change within too short a time period can lead to an explosion.[5]

Leadership often requires pacing the work in order to deal with change at a rate people can stand. Leaders need to remember that groups work best within a range of stress. If the tension is too little, there is no growth; if too great, there is too much anxiety for constructive change. Heifetz and Linsky call this span the "productive range of distress." A task for leaders is that of "controlling the temperature" in either direction. Leaders need to "raise the heat" or "lower the heat," depending on the current status of the change process. An illustration of raising the temperature is drawing attention to tough questions. A way to lower the temperature is to break the problem into more manageable units for further work or otherwise find ways to pace the hard work to make it more emotionally tolerable for the group.[6]

Change is disturbing when it is done to us, exhilarating when it is done by us.
Rosabeth Moss Kanter[7]

NEED FOR PLANNING

The old cliché of "plan the work and work the plan" is strikingly true when a congregation is implementing a new vision. Churches that renew not only go through the spiritual discernment process of identifying God's vision for them, they also develop a plan to achieve the vision. Some lose energy and passion when visioning turns to the more mundane work of organizing for implementation. Both tasks are spiritual tasks of the highest order. Neither is more sacred than the other. Once we are clear about the "treasure" of the gospel God is most calling us to in the immediate future, we do have to give attention to the "earthen vessels" required for its transport.

The biblical term "steward" may be of help here. The steward was a household administrator, but this administrative sense of steward cannot be pressed too far because, in scripture, it was always conditioned by and operated within the terms of the gospel. The administrative dimension of God's work can never be separated from the gospel that informs it. The more administrative aspects of fulfilling

God's vision for a church are to be as spirit filled as the prayer and scripture study that led to the vision in the first place. Stewards are not "ecclesiastical civil servants," to use C. K. Barrett's phrase, but bearers along with others of the riches of God's people in the days ahead.[8]

Jürgen Moltmann captures the relationship between visioning for the future and planning for the future. Unless hope is roused and is alive (through what we are describing as discerning God's vision), there can be no stimulation for planning, he says. However, "without planning, there can be no realistic hope."[9]

Spiritual visioning and practical planning create a strange paradox for the church. On the one hand, visioning normally provides a vision for which there are no assurances of success or mechanisms in place to implement the necessary changes. In that sense, a vision always represents a leap of faith. One can imagine what the future will look like if the vision becomes a reality, but at the moment of vision, there is no way to see the process that will lead to that preferred future. On the other hand, there is something about a vision that draws unto itself the people and processes needed for its implementation. Even while carefully planning the first steps, one has no idea what the next steps will be. One goes forward in faith. Christian leaders know both the importance of careful planning and the limits of planning. We must always be open to adjustment and to the working of God's spirit in unexpected ways during the entire venture.

There is not a neat division between visioning and planning for the vision's implementation. It is not a matter of moving from visions to goals and objectives. The passion and openness to God's spirit must remain always present even as goals, timelines, assignments, and evaluation are in place.

A vision without execution is an hallucination.

Jeffrey E. Garten[10]

THE VISION AS THE CONGREGATION'S COMPELLING STORY

We remember that the vitality of a church lives in the minds of its members. It is out of their story that our new vision has emerged. That story provides the bridge from one chapter to the next. Now the revised story of the next chapter has to become incorporated into the fabric of the congregation. The next chapter's story will continue to be tied to the long history of the people of God, to the denominational heritage of the congregation, to the history of this church, and to what God has in mind for a particular people at a particular time.

A story gives a picture that can be remembered. It touches the spiritual and emotional sides of members as well as the rational. It inspires and challenges. It reminds people where we have been, where we are now, and where, with the help of God, we are going. It gives a sense of progress and provides markers along the way.

It is the story, finally, that makes the difference in churches. The difference from one church to another is not found necessarily in their daily activities. One may be in a maintenance mode and the other may be vital, yet an objective tally of the types of daily activities may not differ significantly. Worshiping, praying, singing, meeting, calling, handling finances, studying, and many other activities may be held in common by the two churches. But what a tally of mere categories of activities can never show is the story in the minds of those who engage in those activities. The work of vital churches may appear as "ordinary" as that of any church, but the story in the minds of its members is such that the whole world of the vital church is utterly different.

It is the story that keeps people going when they are tempted to quit. It is the story that gives energy for that extra effort in the midst of weariness. The story guides and motivates everything that is done. It is the story that gives people

117

a glimpse of the Promised Land and makes the struggle of the journey worthwhile. Leaders not only work with others in discerning that story, the vision, but also tell it because the story means everything to the pilgrimage to the next chapter.

THE LEADER AS STORYTELLER

Howard Gardner, in his study of influential change leaders of the twentieth century, found that "a key—perhaps *the* key—to leadership . . . is the effective communication of a story." The story is key for him because it calls attention to the "common core" and reminds people of who they are. Stories are finally about identity and purpose. For example, he found that in the story that Martin Luther King, Jr., lived and told, there were four primary elements—Christianity, the church, other traditions, and American ideals. "Like a masterful artist," Gardner says, "King was able to draw on and combine these elements in myriad ways, ways that were appropriate to a given situation, ways that involved and energized those who witnessed what he said, ways that resonated with one another and culminated in a more convincing story."[11]

Visions come from many sources. Visions may be identified and named by anyone in a group. As described earlier, leaders are intimately involved in visioning but not the sole players. However, once a vision is clear, it does fall to leaders to be the primary steward of that vision. Leaders keep a vision before the people at all times. Thus, the role of communication is crucial if the plot is to be advanced. "Leadership, in some ways, is like teaching third grade," says Max De Pree; "it means repeating the significant things."[12]

Leaders continually lift the vision and remind people of the story that informs all their endeavors. Churches, like other organizations, have a tendency over time to set up shop for themselves and to become ends in themselves. They

118

forget the motivating story that brought the church into being in the first place. Merely administering and managing such a church will prolong it but will not lead the church into its next generation of life. Rob Weber calls for leaders to become "ImageSmiths" who "create a community of storydwellers and storytellers."[13]

"The essence of leadership—what we do with 98 percent of our time—is communication," says Peter Senge. "To master any management practice, we must start by bringing discipline to the domain in which we spend most of our time, the domain of words."[14] Words have power. They can be used to tear down or for "building up" so that words indeed become a means of grace (Eph. 4:29). Words can lead to despair or to renewed hope. "Your words have supported those who were stumbling," according to Job 4:4, "and you have made firm the feeble knees."

As Senge reminds us, we are communicating all the time. The question is how we shape that communication to advance God's discerned vision for the congregation. While some of the important speaking takes place in large public venues, most communication is of much shorter duration and involves everyday conversations with individuals or small groups. Effective leaders find every opportunity—from sermons to announcements, from annual reports to welcoming visiting groups—to remind everyone of the vision, to motivate for its fulfillment, and to help the story become a part of the vocabulary of everyone.

Edwin Friedman spent many years applying family systems theory to the work of churches and synagogues. He tells about a hotline that was established where pastors and rabbis could call with whatever problem they were having. Friedman and others would help them think through the problems. After doing this for a while, Friedman says when someone called him about a problem, whether it was a problem with the choir or staff conflict or Sunday school issues, he would say at the outset, "Don't tell me your problem. I

119

don't need to know what it is. I am going to give you a solution, and if you will do what I suggest, it will work." He claims that his formula worked in 80 percent of the cases. His solution: "Go back and preach an 'I Have a Dream' sermon."

Friedman was not saying for them to go back and use the pulpit as an opportunity to promote a narrow political ideology disguised as preaching, or to use the pulpit to advance a personal pet project. He was saying, "Go back and remind the congregation of who they are and what they are about. Remind people of the richness of the faith and, thereby, put whatever problems there may be in their proper perspective." I also think this suggestion worked because it helped remind the clergy of who they are. Perhaps they had become caught up in being managers of the conflicts of an institution, and they remembered they are a part of God's great work in the world. They remembered that they are stewards of the richness of the gospel, not ecclesiastical civil servants. Telling the story is powerful indeed.

I was interested to read an article in the *Harvard Business Review* speaking of leadership in the business world. The writer said that she had discovered the hard way in her own company that "a leader's greatest obligation is to preach."[15] She discovered that her personal passion, energy, and drive were important but not enough. She had a larger responsibility to help the entire organization feel a sense of such excitement for their work.

STAY ON MESSAGE

Leaders do not worry about redundancy. Just when someone cannot bear the thought of saying the same things yet another time, most people are just beginning to take it in. Redundancy is essential, though effective communicators find new ways to tell the same story. In a sense, if the story is the tune, the leader finds ways to write different stanzas for that theme over and over.

It was said of a governor of Ohio, that no matter what the occasion at which he was speaking or what the question posed to him at a press conference, his message was always the same: "Jobs and Prosperity for Ohio." In a similar vein, when George W. Bush was first elected governor of Texas, he defeated the incumbent, Ann Richards. Richards remarked that Bush stayed on message during the campaign so much so that if someone said to him, "What time is it?" he would say, "We must teach the children to read."[16]

Although these are not our models, they do point in a direction from which we can learn without mimicking the controlled manner of a political campaign. For example, a church may be hosting a regional workshop for church school teachers, and the pastor has been asked to come at the beginning of the program and welcome the visiting church school teachers from surrounding churches. Among the gathered teachers are most of the host congregation's teachers who have made local arrangements for this event. A pastor may have done this type of welcome a hundred times before. No prior preparation is required. One could say welcome, happy to have you here, thank those who helped make arrangements, say where the bathrooms are, wish them well, and sit down. However, the effective leader will remember this storytelling role and seeing an opportunity, changes the whole welcome, only slightly, but to great effect.

"On behalf of our own church school teachers who have done much to get ready for today, and the entire membership of Trinity Church, I welcome you. There is one thing you need to know about Trinity that you will soon discover if you talk to any of our members or even walk down the halls of the church. We are a mission church. We exist for others. Mission motivates all that we do. In that vein, we want to be of service to you today and hope that you will share with any of our members that you meet ways in which you are in mission from which we can learn."

The host members there may well smile, nod approval,

and sit up a little straighter. They knew they were a mission church, or at least trying to become a mission church, and these few moments only served to remind them of who they were and to confirm their identity as members of a mission church.

Storytelling is the ultimate leadership tool.
Elizabeth Weil, writer

Any individual or organization serious about creating lasting change must get serious about storytelling.
Bill Shore[17]

LIVE YOUR WAY INTO A NEW WAY OF THINKING

Equally as important as communication of the vision is living out the vision in small and large ways. This gives the congregation an opportunity to live their way into a new way of thinking rather than trying to think their way into a new way of living. It is easy to focus all of our attention on the rational dimension of change and forget that the lived experience of a people may be an even more powerful way to influence the change of thinking that is needed.

Many of us are much more likely to act our way into a new way of thinking than think our way into a new way of acting. Moreover, for all of us, experiencing the changes in actual events reinforces changes in our thinking. Leaders play a crucial role in assuring that their behavior and that of the congregation gives everyone a chance actually to see the vision at work. Stated visions must of necessity be proclaimed long before they have become a reality. Visions pull us forward to become what we have not been. Therefore, words will always run ahead of actions to some extent. It is tempting to proclaim the words of the vision, come to believe the vision is true, and ignore that the actual experience of the congregation does not match the vision. In these circumstances, the vision will never take hold.

"People change what they do less because they are given *analysis* that shifts their *thinking* than because they are *shown* a truth that influences their *feelings*," according to John Kotter. Both thinking and feeling are essential for successful change, "but the heart of change is in the emotions." Kotter suggests that the movement of "see-feel-change" is far more powerful that of "analysis-think-change."[18]

SUPPORT THE VISION AND ALIGN ALL SYSTEMS

Nothing is more exciting than the early days of a new vision. All of our talking and praying centers on the vision we truly believe is God's calling for us in the next chapter of our life as a congregation. In some ways it may feel a bit like what Margaret Wheatley calls the "refounding" of an orga-nization. One can even imagine the excitement and high hopes of those who originally founded the congregation.

Renewal is concerned with the revival in mature organizations of the values, feelings, excitement, and emotional commitment often experienced only in the beginning of an organization's life. Renewal is about the restoration of something of value, something important, that has been either lost or forgotten.

David K. Hurst[19]

At these high moments we remember that the only way in which the original founding dream got off the ground was through careful planning and attention to details. Surely in the early years of the congregation there were those who looked back on the time when they were dreaming and did not have to spend much time with the seemingly ordinary tasks of space, personnel, programs, and finances. There probably were other colleagues who gently reminded such persons that those days were wonderful, but that in those days there were no worship services, Sunday school, youth ministry, or outreach to the community. Implementing visions takes hard and careful planning and work.

The founding president of Saint Paul School of Theology was Don W. Holter. Shortly after being named president of this newly approved Methodist seminary, he went to a regular gathering of other Methodist seminary presidents. When it was time for him to introduce himself, he said, "I am Don Holter. I am president of a seminary with no faculty, no students, and no campus." One of the other seminary executives replied by saying, "And you want to change that?!" There are pros and cons to the early founding days of any organization.

Resources need to be provided for the vision to take hold throughout the congregation. The goal is not to have the vision as a separate entity or as a particular program, but rather to have the vision come alive through every aspect of congregational life in appropriate ways. Personnel issues involve having the right kinds of leadership in place—leaders that understand the vision, are committed to it, and who have the spiritual resources and necessary skills to lead effectively. Providing adequate training and leadership development opportunities will be another key to success.

"WEAR" THE VISION

Leaders must be willing to wear the vision they articulate in the same manner that one wears clothes. This is true for all leaders in any field of endeavor. It is true for parents, for business and labor leaders, and for religious leaders. To the extent that a leader's actions match the vision being advanced, there will be coherence and thus strength. To the extent that there is an inconsistency between the proclaimed vision and the actions of a leader, there will be a lack of credibility for the leader and the vision.

Just as leaders find every opportunity to tell the story of the vision, leaders are always finding ways to symbolize through actions that same vision. A pastor described previously used the welcoming assignment for a gathering of church school teachers to remind everyone that their church is a "mission church." That pastor may also decide that taking a week of vacation to go with one of the church's volunteer mission teams for a week of service to the poor is both a way for him to express Christian discipleship and also send a clear signal to the congregation that the pastor is genuinely committed to a mission church. More people may actually "hear" the mission trip than the words about the importance of mission for the congregation.

RECOGNIZE THE VISION

A helpful rule to keep in mind is to recognize and reward that of which more is sought. Leaders find appropriate ways to celebrate those who are living the vision. If a church's vision is around mission, then having a dedication and blessing service for teams going to do volunteer mission work is one way to recognize those for whom the vision is a reality. Giving opportunities for recognition or reporting by teams when they return is another. Personal conversations and notes of appreciation for those living the vision also encourage people who have captured the vision.

For the same reason, leaders need to help the congregation recognize when actions are inconsistent with the vision. This role has nothing to do with the authority of the leader. It has everything to do with the role of leaders as "stewards of the vision." Violations of the vision need not be occasions for personal conflicts between members and leaders. The issue is between actions and faithfulness to the vision the congregation has discerned to be God's vision for them. If the vision centers on children and all the budget categories related to children are frozen for the next year as other aspects of the budget increase, that is a time for a reminder about the vision that the entire congregation is seeking to serve. Structures, reporting mechanisms, evaluation systems, and information collected are all examples of things that need review in light of the vision. Day by day, the new vision needs to become incorporated into "who we are" as a congregation.

ATTEND CAREFULLY TO RELATIONSHIPS

Simply getting this far in the transformation process is a good sign that attention is being given to a multiple set of relationships within and among the congregation. This is no time to lessen tending carefully the fabric of human relationships that, woven together, make change possible or, if not tended well, may sabotage the vision.

Key Leaders

Who are the people without whom the vision cannot become a reality? This question will guide any leader in understanding a set of relationships that need special support and care. Some people will fit into this group by formal position in the church and others by informal moral authority among the people. Some are identified because of special interest or expertise related to the focus of the vision. Some may even come from outside the congregation because of special help or partnership that will be needed from them. Some may be key leaders for the vision not because they play roles directly related to the vision, but because they carry influence and authority over related areas essential to the vision, such as finances, program leadership, or property matters.

The process of forming this "group" is democratic in the sense that persons are identified not because of *who they are* but because of *what the vision is*. Were there another vision at another time, this constellation of people might be quite different given the focus and needs of the alternate vision. The reason for getting a mental picture of this "group," a group that may never actually form or meet as a group, is not for organizational purposes but for leadership responsibilities. These are the people to whom the congregation is looking for extra service and dedication during this renewal effort. It should follow that they are given comparable attention, support, and consultation throughout each stage of the process.

Stakeholders

Congregations tend to be made up not so much of a collection of individuals as a gathering of various groups with common interests. Some of these groups identify more closely with the vision than others. Some will be more involved than others. But all groups should be included in the vision in every way that is feasible and appropriate. At the same time, great care must be given that the basic needs and expectations of various stakeholder groups are not neglected as new areas are developed more directly related to the vision. A simple process is to identify the various stakeholder groups within the congregation and list what their "stakes" tend to be from their perspective. "What is it that each group has a right to expect from their church?" is one good question to ask. If I were a part of each group, what would I feel I had a right to expect?

Attention then must be given to ensure that during the excitement of the vision implementation, none of the basics that relate to the ministries of the church to all groupings is neglected. The vision may revolve around children. What about older members? For one thing, senior adult ministries leaders might be consulted about how they view what they are doing through the lens of the vision around children. This may be a wonderful opportunity for the older adults to become involved in a way that makes sense for them in the new vision. However, whether that happens or not, care must be given to make sure that the basic ministries for older adults are not ignored or devalued because of the new vision. For example, claiming a prime meeting space on Wednesday afternoons for a new children's ministry may fit the vision; but if that space is normally used by a group of older members and their dislocation is not handled with great sensitivity, there is an invitation for sabotage. It has been said that in nonprofit organizations, no one person or group can decide something and make it happen just because they decided it. On the other hand, the wisdom continues, any one group can usually decide something will not happen and succeed in stopping it.

Skeptics, Critics, and Adversaries

Those who feel they have something to lose in the transformation process will naturally be skeptical, even if not openly critical or adversarial, of the new directions. Some of their worries will never materialize. Others can be neutralized as a source of problems by careful reframing by leaders to help these persons put their concerns in the larger context of the new vision. Special attention does need to be given to those who are still experiencing the change process as "losing" something.

Perhaps the new vision centers on an area of ministry that has been a fairly private preserve of a few in the past. Now many others share in this ministry. Perhaps new leadership has gained prominence around the new vision rendering some traditional leaders as "less needed." In fact, they do have relatively less responsibility and influence. Priority for use of space may need to be rethought. In such instances, even if the most consultative and sensitive approach is taken and the groups moving to different space for the sake of the vision agree to do so, there will still be feelings of loss. There are a myriad of ways in which leaders and others can be sensitive to the feelings of such persons and find ways to affirm them and to wrap them into the new vision. Simply acknowledging their loss goes a long way. Ignoring them will not help.

> *Everybody resists change—particularly the people who have to do the most changing.*
>
> James O'Toole[20]

Skeptics also include the natural "show me" types and those who have some genuine reservations about either the direction of the vision or its chances for success. They are not hostile, just skeptical. Regular, understated, and factual communication about the progress of the vision will stand a good chance of making headway with the skeptics. They really do need to "see" the vision unfold. Skeptics will not come to share others' passion and optimism merely through more discussion. They will normally be moved by results. An example is a vision around reaching children in which the skeptics kept insisting that a church "like us" with only "old people" did not have a prayer of succeeding with such a vision. They would be happy to see the vision succeed; they merely did not see it as realistic. These skeptics will take a giant step from skepticism to believing when they see an impressive group of children leading a portion of a worship service.

Critics and adversaries represent a more difficult challenge. Heifetz and Linsky's advice to stay close to friends and even closer to opponents will serve us well in leading change. "To survive and succeed in exercising leadership," they say, "you must work as closely with your opponents as you do with your supporters." They acknowledge that most of us "cringe" at "spending time and especially taking abuse from people who do not share our vision and passion," but the task is essential.[21]

Some fall into this category as much by temperament as by substance. Normally they will have a long history of an adversarial relationship with the leadership of the congregation or with its pastor in particular. Others will have moved into this category as a result of the visioning process itself. Although clear consensus emerged during the discernment phase that the proposed vision is where God is calling the congregation, some never quite bought in to the new vision and some continued to feel an alternate direction was more fitting. A decision to remain in the community where the church has been for a hundred years and commit to serving that community with all the incumbent challenges such ministry will entail will almost always leave one group convinced that relocation is the best option. Likewise, almost any decision for relocation will leave one group unconvinced and, thus, potential critics and adversaries of the new vision.

A leader does not let the broad consensus from the visioning process, or even substantial or unanimous votes by the governing body of the congregation, lead to the conviction that critics and adversaries should "just get with the program." That will not happen easily and, even though they are a small minority, they do have the capacity to sabotage the new vision if they so choose. Those who criticize and oppose consume disproportionate energy. It is good to remember, as some say, that friends come and go but enemies tend to accumulate.

Leaders also keep in mind the network of family and close friends the adversaries have within the congregation. Those close to them may not share their opposition to the vision, but they do regard these people highly and will become concerned over any appearance of mistreatment of them. There are others in the congregation who may not be personally close to the adversaries but would be concerned about any perceived slights toward them. These considerations become paramount when a leader is challenged, questioned, accused, or even verbally attacked by opponents. The substance of the attack is of little significance at that moment. A leader's response to the attack is what matters, period. The handling of such challenge or abuse will seal a leader's fate not so much with the adversaries involved but with the larger congregation.

Even if the substance of the challenge is not accurate, if the response does not take the high road of leadership, the leader's standing within the congregation will diminish. Does this seem unfair? Is it "just" for a leader to be accused of things and not be able to respond with every resource available? No, but leadership is not fair in this sense. Leaders are held to a higher standard. If a leader responds with the emotion and overreach of the adversary, people will forget what the opponent did but will remember the reaction. There is good news here. If there is an unfair attack on a leader, especially if it is in a public setting, and the response is one of grace and understanding, that leader's regard among the congregation will increase. Such leaders do not appear weak. They are seen as leaders with enough self-confidence and care for others not to respond in kind.

Leaders must prepare for such moments because they will come. Without prior thought about ways in which to respond nondefensively, though clearly and considerately, there is a high likelihood of being too caught up in the surprise and personal affront of the attack to respond well in the moment. Those immediate reactions that are later regretted can never be reclaimed. It is as if an actor has missed a cue in the second act of a play. The play goes on; other actors cover for the missed lines. The actor who missed the lines cannot come back in the middle of act three, turn to the audience, and say, "O yes, I remember the lines now. This is what I meant to say." It will not work. No amount of revisiting the sharp

131

exchange will remove it from the mind of the observers. There is one other piece of good news. Sometimes opponents become allies and supporters of the vision. Most leaders have had the experience of a relationship that begins with a great deal of suspicion and even hostility because of disagreements and later becomes one of genuine respect and mutual support. Maybe these times are rare, but they are frequent enough for leaders not to write off cavalierly persons who oppose them or the vision. It is well to remember the example of Abraham Lincoln's dealings with Seward and Stanton, two men to whom Lincoln became close though both of them originally thought the worst of him.

ALLOW ENOUGH TIME

Decline Has a Long Head Start on Renewal

Years ago, the late Richard Hugo gave some intriguing advice about writing. "If a poem you're struggling with doesn't conclude properly," he wrote, "look a few lines before the end for the trouble: trouble is seldom located where you think."[22] Although we tend to look in the immediate past to find the reasons for current problems, their source is more reasonably found much farther in the past. Just because the broad awareness of a problem is recent does not mean that the problem has not been brewing for a long time.

The causes for decline are normally invisible until the condition gets so bad that the signs are obvious even to the most casual observer. In recent years there have been a number of reports about the deteriorating conditions of bridges in the United States. The American Automobile Association reports that 25 percent of the bridges in the United States are either closed or unsafe. Their declining physical condition has been underway for many years, though only experts examining the bridges could tell that it was happening. However, when bridges begin to collapse and people die as a result, an engineering degree is not required to know there is a problem. In a church, the youth ministry may have been aimless for many years with only a few keenly aware of the situation. Once the church no longer has a youth ministry, the entire congregation knows there is a problem.

Solutions, therefore, take a long time given the great "head start" of decline. Anything that has been neglected costs more in dollars and time to renew. To return to the bridges example, one city found upon inspection that 20 percent of its bridges were unsound. The solution will require the expenditure of $24.5 million a year well into the future while the city's budget now only provides for $8.8 million for bridges.[23]

Long before there are problems obvious to everyone, the foundation of past success may have been lost. Things may have been in serious decline for a long time while still appearing fine because of the legacy of past success and its momentum. Squandering may be a fitting word to describe this loss. The same is true for success. Long before general recognition and affirmation occur, the building blocks are in place and unnoticed by most.

I call this "leadership lag time." The phrase comes from Paul Kennedy's use of the term "lag time" to describe a noticeable historical lag time between a nation's relative economic strength and its world influence.[24]

Just as there is a delay in the causes of decline and the most obvious results of decline, there is generally also a major time delay between beginning to address the concern and seeing the solid results of the changes. Leaders must understand this truth. If not, they will be filled with discouragement and even despair or will keep changing from one quick-fix solution to another in the hope of making rapid changes to an area that has suffered inattention for years and years. Some results of change are obviously visible in the short term. But the lasting changes that accompany congregational transformation do take a long time, especially if the renewal follows a time of neglect.

Leading in light of the inevitable lag time between leadership provided and results shown is not easy for most leaders. Mitchell Waldrop likens it to taking a shower when there is a half-minute delay between adjusting the tap and the hot water reaching you. "If you don't take that delay into account properly," he warns, "you can get scalded."[25]

Allowing adequate time normally means a need for continuity of leadership through the transformation process. This presents a dilemma for congregations in which the pastoral leadership rotates every five years or even more often. The same is true if there is high turnover of key lay leadership. Getting a new vision started is not the same as having the new vision take hold within the heart of the congregation. Unfortunately, changes in leadership often mean that promising new directions lose momentum before they take hold and, subsequently, make it even harder for future renewal efforts to gain the energy and support required to succeed.

No Golden Ages

Congregations in decline often look back nostalgically on a perceived "golden age" in their congregational history that serves as the standard by which all current realities are measured. It is as if, in some miraculous way, all the stars were in proper alignment for that remembered golden chapter in their story. The reality is that there is no such thing as a "golden age." What appear to be golden ages are simply one generation reaping the results of another. They mark the end of an era far more than an era itself.

The real golden ages that produce the results appear more like beginnings—chaotic, hard, and painful. Apparent golden ages should be seen more as an alarm than as an achievement. As Peter Drucker has reminded us, "The time of greatest danger for organizations is at times of success because the reasons for success have normally passed by before success comes." That is why experienced success may be so deceiving.

134

Chapter 7
The Power of Vision

Vision is the "Invisible Leader." Vision is not just another project or emphasis alongside other issues. Nor is it even a priority that stands in front of other tasks. Rather, a vision becomes the lens through which virtually everything else is viewed. It provides a different way of viewing every issue and task.

If the vision established is a powerful shared vision, then the task of leaders is not one of convincing people of the merits of the vision. The power to persuade is in the vision itself. If the vision emerges out of the identity of the church and out of the needs of the internal and external contexts, if it is tied to the historic story of faith and matches the story of the needs of the time, then when people hear of the vision, heads should nod in approval. People should respond by saying, "Yes, of course, that's who we are." Or, "That's what I've been saying we should do for a long time." Or, "It's about time!" The basic task of leadership then, after the establishment of the vision, is ensuring faithfulness to the vision.

The shared vision becomes the congregation's "invisible leader." Invisible leader is a term used by Mary Parker Follett. A traditional understanding sees an organization as a pyramid with the leader or leaders at the top deciding what needs to be done with everyone below accomplishing what has been decided. In the understanding proposed here, the organization is seen as an inverted pyramid. At the top of the inverted pyramid is the vision as the invisible leader. Everyone else finds a place within the pyramid. Leaders are at the bottom of the inverted pyramid seeing their task primarily as keeping everyone focused on the vision and faithful to it. They try to keep any persons or groups from pulling out of the pyramid and setting up shop for themselves or for a competing vision.

Leader and followers are both following the invisible leader—the common purpose. The best [leaders] put this common purpose clearly before their group. While leadership depends on depth of conviction and the power coming therefrom, there must also be the ability to share that conviction with others. . . . And then that common purpose becomes the leader. And I believe that we are coming more and more to act . . . on our faith in the power of the invisible leader. Loyalty to the invisible leader gives us the strongest possible bond of union.
Mary Parker Follett (1868-1933)[1]

This does not mean particularity and diversity are sacrificed within the inverted pyramid. Although the vision is the basic tune for the congregation, there will be many people and groups within the church singing different stanzas of the tune. All the groups within the congregation will have their own visions, though all will be consistent with the overall vision. These particular visions are not competing with the overall vision but are consistent with and supportive of the overall vision. Despite the wide range of diverse expressions of the vision, all are faithful to the common leader, the shared vision.

Questions will begin to change with this understanding of congregational life. No longer will questions be primarily about power, prerogative, or even process and procedures; but rather they will be questions of faithfulness and integrity to the vision. Leaders will come to be seen as stewards of the integrity of the vision instead of promoters for their own agendas. Group leaders will become more than advocates for the interests of their ministry areas; they will become active agents in the fulfillment of the vision. Leaders will be seen as those most serving the vision.

One case study reported in the previous chapter described a church with numerous negative trends that discerned their vision to be "reaching younger people." In past times, this church would have declared this a priority issue and named a task force to do something about it. Their approach now was quite different. No task force was named. No special budget was allocated. Instead, the vision of reaching younger people became the invisible leader guiding the work of every group within the church. All ministry areas were asked to look at their work for the coming year through the lens of "reaching younger people." Each group was asked to develop and report their plans to do their work in the coming twelve months in such a way that they could reasonably expect to reach a somewhat younger constituency in the coming year than in the previous year.

The results were amazing. Music ministry started a new choir for children. Sunday school classes recruited younger members. The nominations committee worked carefully to reduce the average age of church officers through new nominations. Worship began to give attention to the ages of participants in the worship services to involve a broader range of members. The evangelism committee held focus groups with younger members to discover what aspects of the church's ministry resonated with them and which ones needed changes made. Each effort alone was modest. However, the combined effort and the synergy it produced began to change the whole spirit of the congregation.

VISION PERMEATES EVERYTHING

Margaret Wheatley talks about vision permeating organizational space. "Vision statements move off the walls and into the corridors," she says, reaching "every recess in the organization." Wheatley goes on to point out that space is never empty. If the space is not filled by a compelling common vision, a vacuum is created that will be filled.[2] Generally, the space will be filled by several competing, and often contradictory, visions.

When a congregation goes long enough without a compelling and unifying vision, the empty organizational space becomes like the crater of an extinct volcano in which every controversy, dispute, and small issue comes to dwell.

Within the congregation with the vision of reaching younger people are people who have strong theological, social, and political views. At times, these differences have virtually overwhelmed everything else going on in the church. The acrimony seemed to escalate in recent years as the church went further into decline. Some council meetings seemed to be more about debating political views than planning to share God's grace. Now the differences remain, but they no longer take up all the oxygen available in the church. The ideas are still debated, but these debates are no longer the essence of the congregation. Even interpersonal relations among members with differing views are better as they work side by side for a vision they are all convinced is the right one for their congregation.

Wheatley is correct in pointing out that without a coherent vision filling organizational space, we cannot expect coherent organizational behavior.[3] Vision determines behavior. The absence of a vision gives rise to behavior that is less than upbuilding for the Body of Christ.

Then the LORD answered me and said: Write the vision; make it plain.

Habakkuk 2:2*a*

VISION IS A FIELD OF ENERGY

Vision is far more than it appears. Some resist focusing on a vision because they feel that whatever the vision is, it will be too narrow and limiting. Just the opposite is true. What is most limited in any organization is energy and focus. A vision gives both.

An appropriate vision becomes a field of energy that produces many results in its wake that could never be logically predicted at the outset. For example, in early American Methodism the unifying vision stated most succinctly was "to save souls." However, during one century, the Methodists established more than a thousand colleges. Nothing inherent in "saving souls" necessarily leads to founding vast numbers of schools. But the vision became a field of energy out of which not only colleges but countless other expressions of this energy manifested themselves.

"A shared vision is not an idea," says Peter Senge. "It is, rather, a force in people's hearts, a force of impressive power." He goes on to remind us that few, if any, "forces in human affairs are as powerful as shared vision."[4] Once a vision is clear, it comes to have a self-regenerating power that leads beyond what any simple linear predictions of cause and effect can ever calculate.

VISION PRODUCES LEADERS

Out of this energy, purpose, and direction, vision creates leaders in its wake. Leaders emerge everywhere. People who do not see themselves as leaders are actually functioning as leaders as they become captured by the vision. Such emerging leadership is not always tidy, but it is energetic.

A denominational official went for an annual visit to one of the congregations with which he works. Throughout the sanctuary were banners that said "Climbing Jacob's Ladder." The official was familiar with this theme because it was being used in another district of the denomination to promote attendance at Sunday school. When asked about the banners, church members quickly replied that this was their Sunday school theme. "This program is not being done in our district," the church official said. "This is a program of another district."

"We know," the church members said. "We heard about the program and sent a delegation to gather information so we could implement it in our church." At that point, the members brought out worn photocopies of a manual they were using that had the other district's name on it. They did not care whose program it was. They were only interested in finding a way to lead their church school to greater vitality.

Distinctions that matter to traditional leaders do not matter as much to these new leaders. What is missing in these new leaders is a preoccupation with old debates, baggage from the past, and assumptions about what can and cannot be done. What unites these new leaders is a passion for the vision.

VISION PRODUCES MIRACLES

Vision causes people to do what appears by any objective standard to be utterly impossible to do. In recent years the world watched with admiration and celebration as a racially inclusive government replaced the oppressive system of apartheid in South Africa. The election of Nelson Mandela as president, following his many years of imprisonment, marked the beginning of a new era.

As with all success, the reasons go back many years. In 1954 it was decided by the African National Congress freedom movement that a description should be written of what life would be like in a democratic South Africa in which all races shared governance. This document—the Freedom Charter—was to be developed by all the people. For two years people throughout the country—people who had virtually no rights or reason to believe things would ever be better for them—participated in small groups painting this picture of what life would look like if freedom ever came. The Freedom Charter, adopted in 1955, became for them a guiding vision over all the coming decades of struggle, death, and imprisonment.

Vision permits us to see results before we are able to see how the results can be achieved. Vision always comes before processes. The 1995 Northwestern University football team was one of the great success stories of all time for collegiate sports. Here was a school that held the record for the longest losing streak of all major colleges. They had not done well enough to go to a post-season bowl game in forty-seven years. However, in 1995 this team not only had a winning season; it was one of the best football teams in the country and went not just to any bowl game but to the Rose Bowl! Gary Barnett, the Northwestern coach at the time, was asked often about the reasons for these miraculous results. Before the Rose Bowl game, he remarked, "I told the players at the beginning of the season to envision what victory and success would be like— what it would look like, feel like, even smell like!"

Such is the power of a vision that can free us from the tyranny of what is and has been, to the expansive possibilities of what can be with the power of God. If we cannot envision anything different from what we have always known, we cannot change our circumstances. "The inner eye of vision can see what isn't yet there, can reach beyond present circumstances," says Robert Fritz, "and can see what, up to that point, has never been there."[5]

Marian Wright Edelman grew up poor in South Carolina, the child of a preacher. After graduating from Yale Law School, she became the first African American woman admitted to the Mississippi Bar. She later founded the Children's Defense Fund and continues as president of that organization. She tells about the night when she was a child and her father died. He was put in an ambulance, and she climbed in to be with her dying father. She tells it this way: "I was fourteen years old the night my daddy died. He had holes in his shoes but two children out of college, one in college, another in divinity school, and a vision."[6] The vision is everything. It is not our circumstances. It is the vision that has the liberating power in our lives and congregations.

Chapter 8
Persevere

Perseverance is the indispensable competency for lasting change. When Al Gore was vice president, he caused a bit of a stir in remarks that appeared to his critics and pundits as his taking credit for "creating the Internet." The jovial jabs he took because of this overstatement served a good purpose. It reminded people that the Internet is not a recent phenomenon. In fact, the Internet began in 1969. It was only after years of development that it came to public awareness and use. When it did, it appeared as something unheard of one day and the topic of daily conversation the next.

What appeared as an "overnight success" actually took many years to develop. The futurist Paul Saffo says that almost all innovations take about twenty years to become an overnight success!

The same pattern can be seen with leadership. Often writers, artists, or business leaders will come on the scene, gaining major attention for a great achievement. They receive significant recognition, and one cannot help wondering why no one had heard of them before. Where were they? What were they doing? Chances are they were doing the diligent daily work required for their "overnight success."

On the day of the Sugar Bowl football game a few years ago, a newspaper story appeared about John Cooper, the head coach of Ohio State, one of the teams playing in the Sugar Bowl. His team had lost one game that season, dominated the Big Ten Conference, and was now preparing to play in a major New Year's Day bowl game.

The sports writer Joe Posnanski used the occasion to tell something of John Cooper's story. Cooper is from a small town in Tennessee, went to college at Iowa State, and slowly worked his way up in college football. "He was an assistant coach at Iowa State, Oregon State, UCLA, Kansas and Kentucky. He finally got a chance to coach at Tulsa. He won big but couldn't get any other jobs. Kansas passed him over. Missouri looked the other way. He finally got a job at Arizona State, took it to a Rose Bowl, beat Michigan, and, as the old joke goes," says Posnanski, Cooper "was an overnight sensation after 25 years."[1]

So it is with almost all leadership achievements in the church, family, community, or vocation. What seems to outsiders as dramatic, virtually overnight, progress is nearly always the result of years of effort by many people. Those who make a difference in the end are those who understand the price of faithfulness and endurance required for accomplishments that matter and last.

For leaders in the midst of the long years leading to major progress, the days can seem weary, lacking immediate results. Saffo says that for those who are in the *midst* of change, the experience is one of evolution. It is only to those looking later from the outside that the change seems revolutionary.

Lifetime achievements tend to take lifetimes, ours and others'. It took generations to build the great cathedrals. Surely we can allow a matter of years for our transformation efforts.

CATHEDRAL BUILDERS

Perhaps cathedral building is the way we should think about our contributions to the unending work of God through time. Bill Shore today is most associated with a type of social entrepreneurship in which nonprofit organizations develop profit generating components to support their mission. Previously he was an aide to several national politicians.

Shore founded Share Our Strength to address hunger. A major source of their funding comes through commercial ventures with restaurants, as well as with other companies. He wrote a book on this concept a few years ago. His later book, *The Cathedral Within*, builds on this spirit. He calls us to move beyond short-range thinking and solutions and join a larger multigenerational effort to build the communities we desire. He points out that cathedrals take many generations to build. The cathedral of Milan took more than five hundred years for construction. Even then, it was built on the foundation of the original fourth-century cathedral.

Out of the many lessons he learned from studying cathedral builders, there are three of his fundamental principles that give guidance to our work as church leaders seeking to renew God's witness through our congregations.[2]

Devoting your life to a cause you will never see completed need not diminish your effort and dedication.

Cathedral building requires the sharing of strength, the contribution of not just the artisans and experts, but of everyone in the community.

The great cathedrals are built, literally, upon the foundations of earlier efforts.

Pies and Perseverance[3]
(Bama Pie Company in Tulsa, Oklahoma, is a third-generation business. It began with the grandmother of the current generation baking pies in

her small home with her husband selling them around Tulsa. Today Bama is a worldwide distributor of pies. The big break came when the son of the founders, Paul Marshall, convinced McDonald's to add pies to their menu and to buy them from Bama Pie Company. Paul Marshall's story of how his company became the single source supplier of pies for McDonald's is a testimony to perseverance.)

It was eleven o'clock. McDonald's had just opened. I walked in and ordered coffee. "You got any pie?" I asked the manager as he served my coffee.

"No, but I wish we did," he said.

"I'm in the pie business and could furnish you with all the pies you could use. Do you think they'd sell?" I asked.

"You bet, but McDonald's won't let us sell just anything. Why don't you go to the head office in Chicago and show them what you've got?" he suggested. I had planned on returning to Tulsa; but when I reached the intersection of Route 66, I changed my mind and turned north. The sign said: Chicago 127 miles. It was two-thirty in the afternoon when I found the McDonald's offices.

"My name is Paul Marshall and I'd like to see the frozen food buyer," I said nervously.

"You'll need to talk to Al Bernardin. Would you like an appointment?" I suddenly felt like the typical country bumpkin. I should have known I'd need an appointment.

But Mr. Bernardin was able to fit me in.

"I own the Bama Pie Company in Tulsa. One product we make is frozen turnovers. I think McDonald's needs a good dessert, and I'd like to sell it to you."

Al Bernardin told me, that winter day in 1965,

that our turnovers were good, but not what they were looking for. I asked him to allow us to develop a pie to their specifications.

"Well, Paul, we'd be willing to work with you, but I'm certainly not going to promise anything. And I'll just warn you, if you work for ten years trying to come up with a pie that fits our need, you still might not get an order."

"I'm willing to take that chance," I said.

We worked a week before I felt we had perfected the formula. Then I returned to Chicago. "Paul," Al said, "I think your pie tastes fine, but I think the crust needs to be lighter and we want apple slices instead of apple chips."

[We] worked another week and finally came up with the crust and filling I felt sure would please Al. "You're getting closer, Paul," Al said.

I went back and forth from Tulsa to Chicago at least once a week for a year. I had almost come to the point of believing that I could never satisfy McDonald's. Then, Al said, "Paul, I believe this is the best pie in America."

"That's wonderful, Al, but when are you going to buy some?" I asked, in frustration.

Al laughed and said "How about right now?"

EVERYTHING LOOKS LIKE
FAILURE IN THE MIDDLE

A statement by Rosabeth Moss Kanter that has encouraged me over the years is, "Everything looks like failure in the middle." Whether it is rearing a child or repairing a home appliance, everything indeed does look like failure in the middle of the process. No matter the project, there comes a time when everything appears to be in chaos and seems as if it will never come together. It is clearly true for a new ministry initiative. Somewhere in the middle of the effort, we get the feeling that maybe we should never have started the task in the first place. Will it ever come together? Will we do more harm than good? Will all the pieces ever fit together to make something whole?

William Bridges and Susan Mitchell talk about this phase of any leadership effort as the "neutral zone," that time after the decision to attempt something new but before the new is a reality. They compare this to the experience Moses faced in trying to lead during the time in the wilderness. They offer lessons for leaders living between the old and the new.

> *Use the plagues. Problems may be your friend. Do not solve them. They may help convince people that things really do need to change.*
>
> *"Mark the ending." Find ways to mark new beginnings with "boundary events," but do not expect to top the crossing of the Red Sea!*
>
> *"Deal with the 'murmuring.'" What was wrong with Egypt, anyway? In periods of transition, stay in touch with those in transition.*
>
> *"Give people access to the decision makers." Make sure questions and frustrations are heard. A new cadre of judges was needed in the wilderness to narrow the gap between the people and the decision makers.*
>
> *"Capitalize on the creative opportunity." It was in the wilderness, not in the Promised Land, that the Ten Commandments were handed down. It will be in the chaotic middle time that many of your biggest break-throughs occur.*
>
> *"Resist the urge to rush ahead." It seems as though not much is happening in the middle zone, but this is where the transformation is taking place. Don't jeopardize it by hurrying.*
>
> *Understand that special leadership is needed. Moses did not enter the Promised Land. A literal new leader is not always needed, but a new way of leading is required for new circumstances.*[4]

Above all, trust in the slow *work of God. We are quite naturally impatient in every-thing to reach the end without delay. We should like to skip the intermediate stages. We are impatient of being* on the way *to something* unknown, *something* new. *And yet it is the law of all progress that it is made by passing through some stages of instability—and that may take a very long time.*

Teilhard de Chardin[5]

OBEDIENCE AND PATIENCE—TWO
COMPLEMENTARY SPIRITUAL DISCIPLINES

"One Day Our People Will Come"

Maggie Brooke grew up on a small Native American reservation in which nearly everyone older than twelve drank alcohol. After sobering up in her twenties, she spent more than a decade lead-ing her people toward health. Now a grandmother in her forties and a tribal elder, Maggie counsels a steady stream of visitors in her home throughout the day. One evening, she told her visitor about Lois, the woman who first inspired her to try to do something about the alcohol dependency among her people.

"Twenty years ago I used to babysit for Lois, who lived in a neighboring band within our tribe. Once a week I'd go the few miles to her community and take care of Lois's little ones. But after about two months, I started to wonder, 'What could Lois possi-bly be doing every Tuesday night? There's not much to do around here in these villages.' So one evening

149

after Lois left to go to the meeting lodge, I packed up the children and went over to the lodge to find out what she was doing. We looked through a window into the lodge and saw a big circle of chairs, all neatly in place, with Lois sitting in a chair all by herself. The chairs in the circle were empty.

"I was really curious, you know, so when Lois came home that evening, I asked her, 'Lois, what are you doing every Tuesday night?' And she said, 'I thought I told you weeks ago, I've been holding AA (Alcoholics Anonymous) meetings.' So I asked her back, 'What do you mean you're holding meetings? I went over there tonight with the children and looked through the window. We watched you sitting there in that circle of chairs, all alone.'

"Lois got quiet—'I wasn't alone,' she said. 'I was there with the spirits and the ancestors; and one day, our people will come.'"

Lois never gave up. "Every week Lois set up those chairs neatly in a circle, and for two hours, she just sat there," Maggie recalled. "No one came to those meetings for a long time, and even after three years, there were only a few people in the room. But ten years later, the room was filled with people. The community began turning around. People began ridding themselves of alcohol. I felt so inspired by Lois that I couldn't sit still watching us poison ourselves."[6]

"The issue is not essentially change or even progress," says Craig Dykstra, vice president for religion for the Lilly Endowment. "It is faithfulness and perseverance." This statement captures the guiding mandate for all Christian leadership. Dykstra borrows from a quotation used by Eugene Peterson as the title of one of Peterson's books to capture this spirit: "a long obedience in the same direction."[7]

Faithfulness and obedience are important. But so is perseverance in the direction of God's will. Patience in the pursuit of God's vision is not wasted time but an essential spiritual practice. Howard Thurman tells of visiting Canada in the middle of winter for some speaking engagements. His driver was a young medical student. Thurman says he was impressed that, despite the huge snow drifts, the student did not use chains to help the tires move through the snow. The student would make quite a ritual out of each new traveling adventure. First, reports Thurman, he would let the clutch out slowly, applying the gas very gently as he chanted, "Even a little energy applied directly to an object, however large, will move it, if steadily applied and given sufficient time to work." The car did not stall once.

What a marvelous way of thinking of the power of obedience and patience combined. Thurman goes on to say that waiting, rather than inactivity or resignation, is a "dynamic process" that "includes also the quality of relentlessness, ceaselessness and constancy." Patience is for Thurman "a mood of deliberate calm that is the distilled result of confidence."[8]

"We Shall Some Day Be Heeded"

In 1894 on her seventy-fourth birthday Susan B. Anthony went out in dreadfully harsh winter weather to preside over the annual convention of the National American Woman Suffrage Association meeting in Washington, D. C. Delegates gathered at the opera house at the corner of Twelfth and F Streets were anticipating hearing their leader speak. They were not disappointed.

Anthony reminded her colleagues that they were now in their fifth decade of seeking the right to vote for women. She told the assembly:

"We shall some day be heeded, and when we shall have our amendment to the Constitution of the United States, everybody will think it was always so, just exactly as many young people believe that all the privileges, all the freedom, all the enjoyments which woman now possesses always were hers. They have no idea of how every single inch of ground that she stands upon today has been gained by the hard work of some little handful of women of the past."[9]

When the US House of Representatives and US Senate finally approved what was to become the Nineteenth Amendment to the Constitution, after being rejected by every Congress for forty years, Susan B. Anthony had been dead for thirteen years. Elizabeth Cady Stanton, the original drafter of the amendment, had been dead for sixteen years.

NO GUARANTEES

Leaders almost never behold an unbroken string of successes. . . . Indeed, the higher the stakes, and the more daring the vision, the greater the chance of repeated failures. . . . What distinguishes leaders . . . are not the occurrences of reversals of fortune but rather the ways in which they deal with, and recover from, such inevitable constants of their calling.

Howard Gardner[10]

It is easy to romanticize leadership. Surely, God's leader and God's cause triumph in the end, even if a great deal of patience is required. The Bible does not romanticize the fate of either leaders or leadership ventures. There are many times when the vision is rejected, or the leader is rejected, or both. There are other times of great success only to be followed by a later forgetting of God's vision and reversion to past unfaithfulness. It would make a better story, for example, to end the telling of Nehemiah's leading the rebuilding of the wall on the optimistic note of the dedicatory service. That would be good, but it would be out of kilter with a key theological theme with which leaders have to reckon, namely, the constant temptation for people to abandon the covenants they had made and return to practices previously corrected by the diligence of reformers.

How could such relapse occur? Do people not learn from the mistakes of the past? Does a new generation not understand the sacrifices made by those who came before them? Was the work of tireless prophets and reformers in vain? Scripture is filled with stories that testify to this all-too-real human weakness to forget God's vision.

We have no control over what will happen in the future. All we can do is to be faithful within the circumstances God has placed us. We can trust that God will take our efforts, even if not successful or sustainable, and use them for the larger purposes of God's work in the world. We are called to persevere not on the basis of guarantees of ultimate success, recognition, or appreciation but from a sense that our lives are committed to doing God's will and that God takes even tentative and incomplete efforts by us and uses them. We rest finally not in our own power but in the power of God to work through us and others.

If [the vision] seems to tarry, wait for it; it will surely come, it will not delay.
Habakkuk 2:3

STAY ALIVE, KEEP PRAYING, AND KEEP WORKING

Change is hard work. Leadership is hard work. Leadership requires a level of physical, emotional, and spiritual energy most people are not willing to give. The intensity of the passion, focus, and even patience takes its toll. The multiple demands on leaders call for extraordinary durability and vitality. Great care must be taken by leaders to keep themselves physically, emotionally, and spiritually healthy throughout the leadership process. A watchword to keep in mind is the instruction given aboard airplanes regarding the use of oxygen masks in the case of an emergency. The guidance always given by the flight attendant is "to secure your mask before assisting others with theirs." We are of no ultimate good to others if we are not healthy and whole ourselves.

Yet, with all the proper care we take for ourselves, the task of leading change is still challenging. It only becomes impossible if we attempt to lead from our own power alone. Faithful and effective leaders remember that we do not labor alone. It is through alignment with God's purpose and God's power that we are able to endure to the end "still standing."

Cornel West uses the term "subversive joy" to capture a secret capability that people of faith bring to the struggles of life. He uses the word "subversive" because this joy does not fit conventional understandings of how life works. Others cannot understand this joy. In fact, often those who display this subversive joy are the very people who have every reason to despair and give up. It is a joy that has no source obvious to the world.

It is a joy that knows that when the going gets hard, we are sustained by the promises of God. When the way is weary, we keep going. . .

knowing that if the vision seems to tarry, it will surely come

knowing that our God does not faint or grow weary

knowing that those who wait for the Lord shall renew their strength

knowing that we will mount up with wings like eagles

knowing we can run and not be weary

knowing that we can walk and not faint

knowing that when we walk through the deep waters, God will be with us

knowing that when we pass through the rivers, they shall not overwhelm us

knowing that when we walk through the fire, we shall not be burned

and knowing with all our hearts that in due season (whenever that may be) we shall reap, if we faint not.

Stay alive, keep praying, and keep working.

Appendix:
Other Visioning Models

While not an exhaustive list, these resources offer creative alternative models for visioning.

CONGREGATIONS ADAPTING TO CHANGE

Carl S. Dudley and Nancy T. Ammerman, *Congregations in Transition: A Guide for Analyzing, Assessing, and Adapting in Changing Communities* (San Francisco: Jossey-Bass, 2002)

Two of the wisest students of congregational life and change have put together an eminently useful guide and workbook for congregational assessment and revisioning. Viewing congregational change as a journey not unlike the journey of the people of Israel described in Exodus, they lay out steps and resources for careful description and planning. The biblical imagery and framework are helpful. One can get a sense of the movement of their suggested planning through chapter titles: Getting the Lay of the Land, Sizing Up Your Tabernacle, Looking for Pillars of Fire, and Across the Jordan: Settling in the Promised Land. Churches of all denominations and sizes will find their book useful.

VISION AS A CONSTELLATION OF STARS

George B. Thompson, Jr., *Futuring Your Church: Finding Your Vision and Making It Work* (Cleveland: United Church Press, 1999)

Thompson uses the metaphor of a constellation of stars to convey something of the quality and power of vision. When we look into the night sky, we see light from stars. We have named the shapes and figures made by the stars. The stars do not arrange themselves in these patterns. These patterns take shape in our minds.

A church's vision is like a constellation. A grouping of stars creates a shape and story for the future that makes sense. Thompson maintains that the stars for creating a compelling congregational vision derive from three sources. All three must be seen in their interrelationships.

Heritage: all the elements of the congregation's past; its own particular history as well as that of the ecclesiastical tradition that gave it birth.

Context: everything that surrounds and permeates the congregation's environment, both the measurable features we see in census reports and the sometimes-elusive features of culture.

Theological bearings: the way in which the congregation orients itself in light of its understanding of what God is like and how God acts; these bearings are both explicit and implicit.

Thompson outlines a visioning process to be completed over approximately one year.

CONGREGATIONAL TRANSFORMATION MODEL

Jim Herrington, Mike Bonem, and James H. Furr, *Leading Congregational Change: A Practical Guide for the*

Transformational Journey (San Francisco: Jossey-Bass, 2000)

These authors have developed a compelling visioning model out of their experiences. The model has three major interdependent and interactive components: spiritual and relational vitality, an eight-stage process for change, and four essential learning disciplines.

Their plan is not for the faint of heart. It is intended for those who understand the need for and desire a comprehensive reorientation of their congregations and are willing to invest the time and effort for such a transformation. They estimate that deep changes may take five to seven years or even longer to accomplish. A companion workbook, *Leading Congregational Change Workbook* (San Francisco: Jossey-Bass, 2000), is valuable.

THE SOUL OF THE CONGREGATION

Thomas Edward Frank, *The Soul of the Congregation: An Invitation to Congregational Reflection* (Nashville: Abingdon Press, 2000), 161-80

On the other end of the spectrum in terms of time involved is a plan that Tom Frank has used with many congregations. The techniques described help to get at the distinctive congregational culture that is the overall subject of his book but also lead to specific next steps in various ministry areas for the church. This model will fit planning retreats in which near-term plans are important. It will also ensure that such plans are rooted in congregational reflection and analysis.

Notes

Introduction: What Happens When the World Changes?

1. Kevin Kelly, editor of *Wired* magazine, quoted in Tom Peters, *The Circle of Innovation: You Can't Shrink Your Way to Greatness* (New York: Knopf, 1997), 68.

2. James O'Toole, *Leading Change: The Argument for Values-Based Leadership* (New York: Ballantine Books, 1996), 161.

3. Mary Parker Follett, *The New State: Group Organization the Solution of Popular Government* (New York: Longmans, Green and Company, 1918; reprint, University Park, Pa.: Pennsylvania State University Press, 1998), 99.

4. "Strategies for Change Leaders: A Conversation Between Peter F. Drucker and Peter M. Senge," *Leader to Leader* (Fall 2000): 19.

5. Nancy Tatom Ammerman, *Congregation and Community* (New Brunswick, N.J.: Rutgers University Press, 1997), 63.

6. Ibid.

7. "Change is Changing," *Harvard Business Review* (April 2001): 125.

8. Ibid.

9. "Strategies for Change Leaders," 19.

10. "Change: Where to Begin," *Harvard Business Review* 69, no. 4 (July-August 1991): 8.

11. Debra E. Meyerson, *Tempered Radicals: How People Use Difference to Inspire Change at Work* (Boston: Harvard Business School Press, 2001), 13.

12. Bill Shore, *The Cathedral Within: Transforming Your Life by Giving Something Back* (New York: Random House, 1999), 181.

1. First Create Trust

1. James M. Kouzes, *Achieving Credibility: The Key to Effective Leadership*, (New York: Simon & Schuster, 1995), cassette.

2. Francis Fukuyama, *Trust: The Social Virtues and the Creation of*

Prosperity (New York: Free Press, 1995), 27-28.

3. O'Toole, *Leading Change*, xvii.

4. Helen Doohan, *Leadership in Paul* (Wilmington, Del.: Michael Glazier Publisher, 1984), 59.

5. Ibid.

6. Carol Hymowitz, "Five Main Reasons Why Managers Fail," *Wall Street Journal*, 2 May 1988.

7. Ronald A. Heifetz and Marty Linsky, *Leadership on the Line: Staying Alive Through the Dangers of Leading* (Boston: Harvard Business School Press, 2002), 75.

8. James M. Kouzes and Barry Z. Posner, *Credibility: How Leaders Gain and Lose It, Why People Demand It* (San Francisco: Jossey-Bass, 1993); Margaret J. Wheatley, *Leadership and the New Science*, Carlsbad, Calif., CRM Films, 1993, videocassette.

9. James M. Kouzes and Barry Z. Posner, *The Leadership Challenge*, 3rd ed. (San Francisco: Jossey-Bass, 2002), 399.

10. *Transformational Leadership for the Healing Ministry: Competencies for the Future* (St. Louis: Catholic Health Association of the United States, 1994).

11. Rosita de Ann Mathews, "Using Power from the Periphery," in *A Troubling in My Soul: Womanist Perspectives on Evil and Suffering*, ed. Emilie M. Townes (Maryknoll, N.Y.: Orbis, 1993), 101.

12. Burt Nanus and Stephen M. Dobbs, *Leaders Who Make a Difference: Essential Strategies for Meeting the Nonprofit Challenge* (San Francisco: Jossey-Bass, 1999), 231-32.

13. Jackson W. Carroll, *Mainline to the Future: Congregations for the Twenty-First Century* (Louisville: Westminster John Knox Press, 2000), 86, italics added.

14. Peter Block, *Stewardship: Choosing Service over Self Interest* (San Francisco: Berrett-Koehler, 1993), 6.

15. Garry Wills, *Certain Trumpets: The Call of Leaders* (New York: Simon & Schuster, 1994), 17.

16. Peg C. Neuhauser, *Corporate Legends and Lore* (New York: McGraw-Hill, 1993), 102.

2. Define Your Congregation's Reality

1. "Exploring Off the Map" Conference sponsored by Leadership Network, May 23-26, 2000, Broomfield, Colorado. The positive potential of accurately naming the truth is captured in a phrase associated with the sociological perspective of symbolic interactionism—"If [people] define situations as real, they are real in their consequences." William I. Thomas and Dorothy Swaine Thomas, *The Child in America* (New York: Knopf, 1928), 572. Thanks to John Verburg for assistance in identifying this reference.

2. O'Toole, *Leading Change*, 169-170, "collective suppression of real-

ity" is from Evans-Pritchard and Polanyi, and British War Office is from Herbert Asquith.

3. Lyle E. Schaller, *44 Questions for Congregational Self-Appraisal* (Nashville: Abingdon Press, 1998), 19-20.

4. "Leading a Congregation Through Change," Symposium on Worship and the Arts, Calvin Institute of Christian Worship, Calvin College and Calvin Theological Seminary, January 11, 2002.

5. Mary Parker Follett, *Creative Experience* (New York: Longmans, Green and Company, 1924), 6.

6. Parker J. Palmer, *Leading from Within* (Indianapolis: Indiana Office for Campus Ministries, 1990), 4.

7. Frederick Buechner, *Telling the Truth: The Gospel as Tragedy, Comedy, and Fairy Tale* (New York: Harper & Row, 1977), 17.

8. Peter Senge, et al., *The Dance of Change: The Challenges of Sustaining Momentum in Learning Organizations* (New York: Doubleday, 1999), 16.

9. Cynthia Woolever and Deborah Bruce, *A Field Guide to U.S. Congregations* (Louisville: Westminster John Knox Press, 2002), 3.

10. George B. Thompson, Jr., *How to Get Along with Your Church: Creating Cultural Capital for Doing Ministry* (Cleveland: Pilgrim Press, 2001), 67.

11. Ibid., 68.

12. O'Toole, *Leading Change*, 258.

13. For Hamilton's account of the remarkable story of the development of the Church of the Resurrection, see *Leading Beyond the Walls* (Nashville: Abingdon Press, 2002).

14. Heifetz and Linsky, *Leadership on the Line*, 134-39.

3. Discern a Vision

1. Lillian Hellman, *Pentimento* (New York: New American Library, 1973).

2. Willie Morris, *My Mississippi* (Jackson, Miss.: University Press of Mississippi, 2000), xv, 80. The Lillian Hellman quotation is from *Pentimento* (New York: New American Library, 1973).

3. A. N. Whitehead, quoted in Warren Bennis, *An Invented Life: Reflections on Leadership and Change* (Reading, Mass.: Addison-Wesley, 1993), 28.

4. Fintan O'Toole, quoted in Mary Bray Pipher, *Another Country: Navigating the Emotional Terrain of Our Elders* (New York: Penguin Putnam, 1999), 58.

5. Thompson, *How to Get Along*, 6-10. Thompson is drawing upon the work of Edgar H. Schein, *Organizational Culture and Leadership*, 2d ed. (San Francisco: Jossey-Bass, 1992), chapter 2.

6. Ibid., 11.

7. Ibid., 10-20.

8. Ibid., 20.

9. Edgar H. Schein, *The Corporate Culture Survival Guide: Sense and Nonsense About Culture Change* (San Francisco: Jossey-Bass, 1999), 189.

10. Ibid., 191.

11. John W. Gardner, *On Leadership* (New York: Free Press, 1993), xi.

12. R. Robert Cueni, *Dinosaur Heart Transplants: Renewing Mainline Congregations* (Nashville: Abingdon Press, 2000). Specific excerpts from the book will be referenced as used. However, much of what I learned from Cueni's research came from informal conversations. His conclusions match my own experience and what I have seen in the renewal of many long-existing congregations. At the time of his research and writing, Cueni was pastor of Country Club Christian Church in Kansas City, Missouri, a large Disciples of Christ congregation with an impressive building. Cueni points out that the name of the church refers to the name of a neighborhood, not their mission! He is now president of Lexington Theological Seminary.

13. Leander Keck, *The Church Confident* (Nashville: Abingdon Press, 1993), 65.

14. Cueni, *Dinosaur Heart Transplants*, 18.

15. Ibid., 19.

16. George B. Thompson, Jr., *Futuring Your Church: Finding Your Vision and Making It Work* (Cleveland: United Church Press, 1999), 30.

17. Ibid., 31.

4. Identify Key Phases of Your Visioning Process

1. Some resources in dealing with organizational life cycles are listed here. For business organizations, see John P. Kotter, *The Leadership Factor* (New York: Free Press, 1988), 57-62; Noel M. Tichy and Mary A. Devanna, *The Transformational Leader* (New York: John Wiley & Sons, 1986), 27ff.; James C. Collins and William C. Lazier, *Beyond Entrepreneurship* (Englewood Cliffs, N.J.: Prentice Hall, 1992), 102, 115. For congregations, see Martin F. Saarinen, *The Life Cycle of a Congregation* (Alban Institute, 1986). For denominational cycles, see David A. Roozen and C. Kirk Hadaway, eds., *Church and Denominational Growth* (Nashville: Abingdon Press, 1993); C. Kirk Hadaway and David A. Roozen, *Rerouting the Protestant Mainstream* (Nashville: Abingdon Press, 1995); Roger Finke and Rodney Stark, *The Churching of America 1776-1990* (Brunswick, N.J.: Rutgers University Press, 1992); Nathan O. Hatch, *The Democratization of America* (New Haven, Conn.: Yale University Press, 1989); Wade Clark Roof and William McKinney, *American Mainline Religion* (Brunswick, N.J.: Rutgers University Press, 1987).

2. Burt Nanus, *Visionary Leadership: Creating a Compelling Sense of*

Direction for Your Organization (San Francisco: Jossey-Bass, 1992), 16.

3. Denise G. Shekerjian, *Uncommon Genius: How Great Ideas Are Born* (New York: Penguin, 1990), 170.

4. Craig R. Hickman and Michael A. Silva, *Creating Excellence* (New York: NAL Books, 1984), 151.

5. Nanus, *Visionary Leadership*, 135.

6. Margaret J. Wheatley, "Innovation Means Relying on Everyone's Creativity," *Leader to Leader* (Spring 2001): 17.

7. James O'Toole, *Leadership A to Z: A Guide for the Appropriately Ambitious* (San Francisco: Jossey-Bass, 1999), 192-93.

8. Mark Olshaker, *The Instant Image* (New York: Stein & Day, 1978).

9. Michael J. Kami, *Trigger Points* (New York: McGraw-Hill, 1988), 89.

10. *Presidential Power and the Modern Presidents: The Politics of Leadership from Roosevelt to Reagan*, 3rd ed. (New York: Free Press, 1990), 129, in Ronald A. Heifetz, *Leadership Without Easy Answers* (Cambridge, Mass.: Belknap Press of Harvard University Press, 1994), 193.

11. Parker J. Palmer, *Leading from Within: Reflections on Spirituality and Leadership* (Indianapolis: Indiana Office for Campus Ministries, 1990), 15.

12. Nan Stone, "Ideas to Steer By," *Harvard Business Review* 73, no. 4 (July-August 1995): 18.

13. Margaret J. Wheatley, *Leadership and the New Science*, Carlsbad, Calif., CRM Films, 1993, videocassette.

14. M. Mitchell Waldrop, *Complexity: The Emerging Science at the Edge of Order and Chaos* (New York: Simon & Schuster, 1992), 12.

5. A Model for Visioning

1. This is not the only way to define *mission* and *vision*. Some persons actually use these two terms in just the opposite manner from the way I have defined them, with *vision* representing the larger goal and *mission* the specific achievements needed to achieve the vision. An example of this usage can be found in Thompson, *Futuring Your Church*, 7. It is important not to let terminology become a problematic issue. The words are not essential, but the meaning addressed by the words is. These realities can be named in whatever ways make sense, always being sure to clarify both purpose and also that to which God is most calling the congregation in the near future based on that purpose and current circumstances.

2. Richard Southern and Robert Norton, *Cracking Your Congregation's Code: Mapping Your Spiritual DNA to Create Your Future* (San Francisco: Jossey-Bass, 2001), 24.

3. Thomas Edward Frank, *The Soul of the Congregation: An Invitation to Congregational Reflection* (Nashville: Abingdon Press, 2000), 66.

4. Harry Levinson, *Executive: The Guide to Responsive Management* (Cambridge, Mass.: Harvard University Press, 1981), 105.

6. Take the Next Step

1. Thompson, *Futuring Your Church*, 31.
2. "David's Eyes," National Public Radio's *All Things Considered*, June 13, 2000.
3. Harvey Robbins and Michael Finley, *Why Change Doesn't Work: Why Initiatives Go Wrong and How to Try Again—and Succeed* (Princeton, N.J.: Peterson's, 1996), 11.
4. "Exploring Off the Map" Conference.
5. Donald L. Laurie, *The Real Work of Leaders* (Cambridge, Mass.: Perseus, 2000), chapter 9.
6. Heifetz and Linsky, *Leadership on the Line*, 107-16; see also Heifetz, *Leadership Without Easy Answers*, 241-46.
7. Rosabeth Moss Kanter, *The Change Masters* (New York: Simon & Schuster, 1983), 63.
8. C. K. Barrett, *A Commentary on the First Epistle to the Corinthians* (New York: Harper & Row, 1968), 100.
9. Jürgen Moltmann, *Hope and Planning*, trans. Margaret Clarkson (New York: Harper & Row, 1971), 178.
10. Jeffrey E. Garten, *The Mind of the C.E.O.* (New York: Basic Books, 2001), 133.
11. Howard Gardner, *Leading Minds: An Anatomy of Leadership* (New York: Basic Books, 1995), 62, 209-10.
12. Max De Pree, "Visionary Jazz," *Leadership*, XV, 3 (Summer 1994): 18.
13. Rob Weber, *Visual Leadership: The Church Leader as ImageSmith* (Nashville: Abingdon Press, 2002), 18.
14. Peter M. Senge, "The Practice of Innovation" *Leader to Leader* (Summer 1998): 17.
15. Kye Anderson, "The Purpose at the Heart of Management," *Harvard Business Review* (May/June 1992): 61.
16. *Kansas City Star*, 2 August 1999.
17. Shore, *The Cathedral Within*, 199.
18. John P. Kotter, *The Heart of Change: Real Life Stories of How People Change Their Organizations* (Boston: Harvard Business School Press, 2002), 1-3.
19. David K. Hurst, *Crisis and Renewal: Meeting the Challenge of Organizational Change* (Boston: Harvard Business School Press, 1995), 1.
20. James O'Toole, *Leading Change*, 13.
21. Heifetz and Linsky, *Leadership on the Line*, 87.
22. Peter Davison, "Finding Time to Write," *The Key Reporter*, Phi Beta Kappa newsletter (Spring 2001): 4.
23. Jeffrey Spivak, "Nearly 20 Percent of KC Bridges Are Found Unsound," *Kansas City Star*, 14 June 1996.

24. Paul Kennedy, *The Rise and Fall of the Great Powers* (New York: Random House, 1987), xxiii.
25. Waldrop, *Complexity*, 25.

7. The Power of Vision

1. Mary Parker Follett, *Freedom and Co-ordination* (London: Management Publications Trust, 1949), 55. For more on the role of vision in leadership, see Lovett H. Weems, Jr., *Church Leadership: Vision, Team, Culture, and Integrity* (Nashville: Abingdon Press, 1993), chapter 2.
2. Margaret J. Wheatley, *Leadership and the New Science*, 2nd ed. (San Francisco: Berrett-Koehler, 1999), 54-58.
3. Ibid.
4. Peter M. Senge, *The Fifth Discipline: The Art and Practice of the Learning Organization* (New York: Doubleday, 1990), 206.
5. Robert Fritz, *The Path of Least Resistance* (Salem, Mass.: Stillpoint Publishing, 1984), 67.
6. Marian Wright Edelman, *The Measure of Our Success: A Letter to My Children and Yours* (Boston: Beacon Press, 1992), 7.

8. Persevere

1. Joe Posnanski, "Buckeyes Can Take Toll on Coach," *Kansas City Star*, 1 January 1999, D1.
2. Shore, *The Cathedral Within*, 19-20. Shore's previous book on social entrepreneurship is *Revolution of the Heart* (New York: Riverhead Books, 1996).
3. Adapted from Paul Marshall with Brian and Sandy Miller, *A Piece of the Pie* (privately printed, 1987), 1-4, 202-4.
4. William Bridges and Susan Mitchell, "Lessons from the Wilderness," *Leader to Leader* (Spring 2000): 3.
5. From *THE MAKING OF A MIND* by Pierre Teilhard de Chardin. Copyright © 1961 by Editions Bernard Grasset. English translation copyright © 1965 by William Collins Sons & Co., Ltd. London and Harper & Row, Inc., New York.
6. The original source of this story is Sousan Abadian, "From Wasteland to Homeland: Trauma and the Renewal of Indigenous Communities in North America" (Ph.D. dissertation, Harvard University, 1999). This version from Heifetz and Linsky's *Leadership* has been adapted with names changed and other alterations to maintain confidentiality.
7. Craig Dykstra, "A Long Obedience in the Same Direction," *Initiatives in Religion* 5, no. 2 (Spring 1996): 2.
8. Howard Thurman, *Deep Is the Hunger: Meditations for Apostles of Sensitiveness* (Richmond, Ind.: Friends United Press, 1951, reprinted 1990), 53-54.
9. Lynn Sherr, *Failure Is Impossible: Susan B. Anthony in Her Own Words* (New York: Times Books, 1995), xi.
10. Gardner, *Leading Msinds*, 218.

Key Name Index